Danni Carr & Ash Grunwald

HOW I QUIT ALCOHOL
A ROCK 'N' ROLL GUIDE TO SOBRIETY AND LIVING WELL

iquitalcohol.com.au

Published in 2024
© Danni Carr & Ash Grunwald
Edited by Katelyn Rew
Danni Carr photo by Tree Faerie
Ash Grunwald photo by Mos & Co
Cover & Text design by Donna Gee

Paperback ISBN: 978-0-646-89794-3

The information contained in this book is for general purposes only. It is not intended as and should not be relied upon as medical advice. A medical practitioner should be consulted if you have any concerns about your mental or physical health.

All rights reserved. No part of this publication may be reproduced, stored in a retrieval system, or transmitted in any form or by any means, electronically, mechanical, photocopying, recording or otherwise, without the prior permission of the copyright owners and the publishers.

For our 'WHY,' Sunny and Aria
xx

CONTENTS

INTRODUCTION	01
01. THE TRASHBAG Danni's Story	07
02. ROAD DOG Ash's Story	25
03. IN THE FOOTSTEPS OF MY HEROES	41
04. THE ALCOHOL INVERSION THEORY	55
05. THE BINGE DRINKER'S TREADMILL	69
06. EXCUSES, EXCUSES	81
07. CONFESSIONS OF AN INSTIGATOR	93
08. THE THIEF & THE BROTHEL	105
09. I'VE GOT A BURNING DESIRE	119
10. POISON IN THE PUNCH	131
11. HANGXIETY	145
12. THE POWERS THAT BE	157
13. LEAVING THE CULT	169
14. MENTORS & MINDSET	181
15. RUN OR RISE	193
16. FEELING THE FEELS	203
17. BRINGING IT ALL BACK HOME	215
ACKNOWLEDGEMENTS	225
BOOKS BY THIS AUTHOR	229
ABOUT THE AUTHOR Danni Carr	230
ABOUT THE AUTHOR Ash Grunwald	231

Precautionary warning:

If your drinking is super heavy, you may have developed a physical dependency on alcohol. If this is you, or even potentially you, please get medical assistance and advice if you are planning to stop drinking. Sudden withdrawal from ethanol can be potentially life-threatening. Always speak to your doctor if you have any doubts.

INTRODUCTION

Are you feeling worried about how much you've been drinking lately? Tired of waking up with regrets, piecing together the events of the night before? Perhaps you've tried to moderate, only to find yourself back at square one time and time again. Or maybe you simply want to regain control of your life and become a better parent, friend, or partner.

Well, you're not alone, my friend! Hundreds of thousands of people feel the same way. We know those feelings all too well. We've been there, waking up at three in the morning with cold sweats and a pounding heart, desperately trying to piece together the night before.

Did I offend anyone? Did I make a dick out of myself? How did I get to bed, and worst of all, how did my kids get to bed?

There is literally no worse feeling in the world. The sense of being out of control. Swearing you'd never end up in that situation again, only to find yourself there, ashamed and longing for clarity.

In Australia, alcohol is often sold as the key to having a good time. It's the accepted method of showing hospitality and a readiness to get into it by joining the tribe in a piss-up. Drinking is seen as a gesture of a willingness to enjoy yourself. In fact, in many circles, the bemused refrain, 'What's wrong with you?' is commonly asked of the 'party pooper' seen as boring or straight. Total shock horror! Are they up themselves? Elitist? Are they churchy? Are they on some health kick?

Maybe once upon a time, when you snuck your first teenage sip against your parent's wishes, getting drunk was a little rebellious. Now, twenty years later, slurring away on the same old story, with the same old music in the background, as you hang out with the same old people...well, it's getting a little stale.

It's time to realise that you can still experience good times without using alcohol to mark, celebrate, or commiserate Every. Single. Fucking. Occasion.

People think if they quit drinking, they'll be boring and lose their friends, confidence, charisma and edge. We worried about all of the above, too, and fundamentally questioned whether we would even be able to actually quit! We just didn't see ourselves as non-drinkers and couldn't imagine what that would look like. But we also couldn't deny that alcohol had become a destructive, obstructive and downright dangerous part of our lives.

Throughout this book, we'll show you how we removed the need for booze by changing our mindset and beliefs. As musicians who have been deeply entrenched in the music industry for decades, we've experienced firsthand how the culture surrounding alcohol can impact creativity, sobriety, and mental health.

We'll draw on our experiences and insights to provide practical advice and guidance for anyone looking to break free from the grip of alcohol. You'll get a backstage pass to our lives, with raw and honest firsthand stories that take you behind the velvet curtains of the music industry.

Through these stories, you'll gain a deeper understanding of the challenges we faced and the strategies we used to navigate the journey to sobriety.

We're not therapists and don't hold PhDs in psychology or addiction. But we have spent countless hours in deep regret, anxiety and self-hatred, only to jump on the treadmill again, partying, drinking and blacking out.

We'd go hard on a healthy lifestyle for a while and then find ourselves back in the same situation, waking up hungover and disgusted. We have lived it, felt it, vomited it up, drank it down, and pressed repeat on destructive patterns, triggers and denial, but somehow, we got through to the other side.

When we finally committed to giving up alcohol, our happiness levels went through the roof, and our professional and personal lives began to forge ahead. They improved radically with all the extra time we now had available, and our physical and mental health improved beyond measure. Life is now beautiful, clear, and productive, and the guilt and shame have gone.

We want to show you that it's possible to get yourself out of the binge drinking cycle, and the simple fact is that the harder you find it to quit alcohol, the better it will be for you. If you can't imagine a good time without alcohol, you must read this book!

You can dismantle the limiting self-belief that you need alcohol for a good time. When you do, you'll gain a sense of clarity and control that you may not have experienced for many years. You'll see a marked increase in your optimism, gratitude and zest for life. If you commit to doing the work, you'll experience a change in your relationships, and most importantly, your relationship with yourself.

We'll guide you through the process of challenging your mindset and your relationship with alcohol while also creating new positive and rewarding habits. You'll see that you aren't giving anything up but rather giving yourself an incredible gift. By the end of this book, you should feel transformed and ready to tackle not just alcohol but also any other self-limiting habits and beliefs.

One year from now, you will see results in every area of your life. For us, that first year of sobriety was a magical time. It wasn't without its challenges, but we grew exponentially as people, as a couple and as parents.

Take it from some self-confessed binge-drinking trashbags! Sobriety is the most amazing gift you can ever give yourself, and we can help you to get there. It truly is an incredible place to be.

Sobriety is an act of rebellion, and the sober revolution is well underway. So, buckle up and get ready for an intimate and enlightening ride as we share our triumphs, setbacks, and everything in between.

With heart,
Danni Carr & Ash Grunwald

1.
THE TRASHBAG
Danni's Story

It's eleven in the evening. I've just woken up from a deep sleep. For maybe a second or two, I have that warm, cosy feeling when suddenly confusion hits me. My mouth is dry, and I have no idea what time or day it is. I can smell vomit, and my head is pounding. That anxious feeling, that familiar dread, takes its place in the pit of my stomach, and I begin to sweat. I hear my friends Lex and Corli outside, listening to Elton John. They sound like they're having a good time, but shame hits me like a sucker punch.

This is not how my night was meant to go. Instead of waking up smelling like vomit with a full-body hangover, I was meant to be putting my kids to bed. We'd planned a sleepover for them with their friends to watch movies and eat popcorn. I was meant to be the doting Mum tucking them all in for the night while my friends went out for a romantic dinner. But that's not the scene that is playing out right now. I flashed back to earlier that afternoon. We all met up so I could take the kids home with me, and then someone suggested we have a quick drink. I ordered a Vodka, Lime and Soda, and when the waiter asked if I wanted a double shot, I said, 'Why not?'

Frivolity ensued. I readily forgot my earlier resolutions to not drink, to drink less, to keep it together as the designated person to do the adulting. God knows how many doubles later, and the last thing I recall is falling out of the taxi at my house in the late afternoon and vomiting all over my shoes in front of the kids and my friends.

Then I passed out in bed. I vaguely remember my daughter Sunny coming in and patting my head, feeling sad for me because of the 'bad' food I'd eaten.

How did this even happen? I could cry just thinking about it. I could cry at the shame I felt when I woke up those lost hours later. That feeling that I'd let my friends down, but worst of all, that my kids had seen me like that.

What was I doing to myself? What example was I setting for my kids? And what sort of friend and mother was I? I was so sick and tired of asking myself these same questions again and again. The same story where I told myself what a failure I was and how this wouldn't happen again. The same story where I fooled myself into believing I could really stop the over-drinking, the bingeing, the getting to the black-out stage, the living the lifestyle of a burgeoning alcoholic.

That was the last time I had a serious binge drink.

I'm incredibly thankful for that night because it was the turning point that forced me to take an honest look at myself. A few months later, I made a pact with a group of friends to take twelve months off drinking and set about on a path of self-forgiveness, self-love and discovery.

I have never looked back.

There are so many lost nights that started off as 'a few drinks' with friends before spiralling into evenings of epic out-of-control drunkenness, ending in a blur of inappropriate verbal diarrhoea and raucous behaviour.

I'm a fearless over-sharer by nature (something that I am currently working on), and mixing that with excessive alcohol consumption led to some extremely cringe-worthy moments that still embarrass me to this day.

I would drink and tell endless stories about the internal workings of my marriage, other people's marriages, my deepest secrets, the state of my vagina after childbirth, my sex life, what I ate for breakfast, my opinions about life, and my opinions about other people's lives.

I would leave no stone unturned.

There was no room for people to get to know me. I had zero boundaries and certainly no air of mystery. I realise now that I was, at times, that scary drunk woman who had no filter, who made grandiose pronouncements, who 'spoke her truth,' but I did this with no sensitivity to other people's feelings.

The booze took away any awareness of hurting or offending others. My sensitivities were blunted and diminished, but my confidence was sky-high.

At the time, it all seemed like a bit of fun. Waking up the next day and laughing it off to hide my embarrassment was normal, as was sending out endless apology texts, but I knew something had to change.

A friend sent me a photo a few days ago, taken when we were young, of a particularly drunken fiasco. A photo I would have boasted and laughed about years ago now makes me cringe, and I instantly deleted it.

It's funny how sobriety changes your perspective on things.

I used to own my drunken actions and retell the stories as though they were something I did to be funny, that they were intentional or part of my wild sense of humour. In reality, I was simply trying to justify an action that I just happened to do because I was too drunk.

I knew it wasn't me and that I was misrepresenting myself, but I had a raft of excuses I told myself and others to gloss over the truth. Alcohol was helping me to hide and disassociate from my feelings of inadequacy and insecurity.

I used to hate Sunday mornings, particularly around three, when I would wake from an intoxicated sleep, not knowing what day or time it was. For a moment, I would have a flashback of the afternoon or night before, laughing with friends, dancing with abandon, then maybe vaguer memories of cornering someone for a deep and meaningful chat, then…shit…what came next? What happened?

That feeling of dread would crawl into the pit of my stomach like a snake.

I'd feel like I knew something bad had gone down, but I couldn't recall what it was. I would feel sick and fragile. My bravado of the night before had gone south. I would often shake Ash awake (If he was home from his endless touring) and desperately ask him, 'Did anything bad happen last night?' I would wait for him to fill me in, but poor Ash was coming out of his own intoxicated slumber.

What had transpired the night before? Was I well-behaved? Did someone leave our house feeling offended or uncomfortable? I would look for clues in Ash's voice. Was he annoyed with me? I would then reach for my phone and search through the call list and messages to see who I'd rung and for how long. I'd sigh in relief if it was just a family member I'd called. They knew what I was like. I had made so many of those calls.

If it was another binge drinking mutually enabling friend, I could laugh it off with an apology text. But oh, the cringe when I had called a new acquaintance, a work associate or some unsuspecting celebrity musician who I felt wanted to talk to me at midnight in my 'I'm having a wow of a time' state. It was all so embarrassing and stressful.

I could rarely get back to sleep after that. I would

toss and turn with a pounding head and dry mouth and desperately try to piece together the night before, anxiety causing my heart to thump so hard I thought it would jump right out of my chest.

I later learned there is a term for this - hangxiety. The anxiety you get when you're hungover and don't have a fucking clue what you did the night before. I'd been suffering mild states of hangxiety for decades, and it was only getting worse. What I used to shrug off on the weekends in my twenties was becoming a permanent state for me in my late thirties, and I was sick to death of feeling that way. As I contemplated the looming uncertainty of my future, memories of my upbringing flooded back.

My family were country people. I grew up in the Central Victorian town of Castlemaine, the traditional land of the Dja Dja Wurrung People, also known as the Djaara People. This small town was a major centre in the 1851 gold rush and is about 40km from Bendigo.

I can barely recognise the place now, with its cafes and hipsters.

When I lived there from 1988 until the early 2000s, it was a bit of a backward country town, inhabited by bored teenagers dividing themselves into jocks, skegs, hippies and social outcasts.

The jocks were the sporty types, the footy players who played for Castlemaine. They were douche-brained pretty boys with a pack mentality, full of bravado when they were in the safety of their tribe. They went out with the pretty blonde girls, but mostly they would try to stick their dicks in anything that moved. Don't get me wrong, a couple of these guys were my friends, but they mostly seemed a bit dense, too eager to fight and too eager to down as many drinks as humanly possible while acting like total Neanderthals.

The skegs were the baggy-pant-wearing skaters. These guys were cool and a bit edgy, smoking heaps of pot and doing skater art. They were also players, but they certainly weren't punching on at the end of the night at the Criterion Hotel. The only time you would see them in a fight was if they were trying to dodge a punch to the head by one of the jocks.

The hippies were not unlike the skegs. They wore old man cardigans from the op shop and were probably more inclined to smoke bongs than drink pint after pint of beer.

Our group of friends drank a lot, and when the

weekend rolled around, all there was to do was get wasted. I was scared shitless the first time I drank. I didn't want to do it, and when I did, I wouldn't say I liked it. I have spoken to so many people who said that the first time they drank, the first time their brains got flooded with dopamine from the alcohol, they just loved it. This wasn't the case for me.

Nevertheless, we'd drink ourselves silly, listen to music, cry after a big heart-to-heart, and get up to no good. We were loud, intense and passionate. We'd sneak out of our parents' houses and go to parties. In our oblivion, we'd let our bodies be used by young men who didn't know how to respect young women. They'd make their move on us when we were out of it and vulnerable. On Monday at school, when everybody inevitably learned about it from their bragging, we'd feel humiliated. It fucked with our self-esteem, and we'd be left feeling so ashamed.

Yet it kept happening, weekend after weekend. It was the same old story. We'd sneak out and get someone's brother or sister (or any old dude off the street) to buy us a cask of Fruity Lexia. We'd hit the Western Oval, Victory Park, or often go to our friend Bill's house, as his mum let us drink there.

So, drink we did. At the ripe old age of fourteen, we'd greedily skull that sweet, syrupy cask wine like thirsty explorers coming out of the desert. We'd smoke hydro joints, listen to Cold Chisel, pash some guy, get fingered, drink more goon, usually ending the night in a high-drama D&M, or chasing after one of our friends who would always crack the shits and run off into the night like some wild loony that we couldn't handle.

Our parents had no idea what the hell we were up to. I was the youngest of six, and I think they were well and truly over trying to rein in the behaviour of a teenage girl by then.

★ ★ ★

As we got older and more sophisticated, we upgraded the alcohol-binge house sessions to the Criterion Hotel, a beautiful and grand old building established in 1892. It was a bit creepy. The Badloves wrote a song about the ghosts there.

On the weekends, it'd be heaving with people ready to 'Get on the sauce horse,' a term used by the jocks that meant they were going to drink as much as possible in the space of four hours.

The mix of personalities, the consumption of large quantities of alcohol, and the sheer volume of bodies crammed into the space created a violent tension in the air. Often the guys would be groping girls, sometimes flopping their dicks out. Girls dressed to the nines entered as friends and left dishevelled and wasted, calling each other sluts, bitches and cunts on their way out. There would always, and I mean always, be a fight at the end of the night.

I saw so much blood on the concrete out the front of the Criterion Hotel. I saw people acting like animals, and I never once questioned it.

As the evenings progressed, we'd go to a nightclub called The Pit in the old Theatre Royal building. We'd all stagger up there after being thrown out of the Cri', and then there'd be more fights. Drunken dickhead jocks yelling obscenities to the petrolheads driving past. Someone would be throwing up in Victory Park, pretty girls walking barefoot, faces smeared with mascara. After the Pit spat us out at one in the morning, it would be up to Capones Pizzeria to soak up the alcohol with a family-sized Capricciosa with extra chilli.

At sixteen, I had a boyfriend from the petrolhead set, the guys with hotted-up cars that would do blockies or burn rubber. Round and round like a carnival ride, carving out doughnuts on the road, listening to music from their Bose speakers, drowning out the sounds of the RX4 rotary engines. The girls would drink in the back of their cars before heading to the pub. These guys were on their P plates and didn't drink and drive. They were nice guys, really, and were probably trying to keep us girls out of trouble.

I still have many great friends in Castlemaine, but at the time, I couldn't wait to get out of there. I have terrible memories of that haunted era. All the drinking and abuse. All the friends who checked out way too soon. The way people treated each other - my own shitty behaviour.

I moved away when I was about twenty, but you can never take the country out of the girl, and you sure as shit can't take her binge-drinking culture away, either. New geography didn't change the behaviours that were now well and truly a way of life. As I got older, it just got worse.

Over the years, it changed its outward appearance. I dressed it up as cultured, a sign of sophistication. In my late thirties, I got my 'posh' on and began appreciating life's finer things. So, my taste for expensive wines grew, making me feel a little classier, like I knew what I was talking about. I had money to burn, and when you're buying top-shelf wines or spirits, you feel like you're a bit more dignified than some binge-drinking teenager at the oval.

The reality was far from it. If anything, it gave me the license to drink more. With that came the crippling hangovers and the shame factor. I knew that my behaviour from the night before was anything but a classy affair.

I'd compulsively drink to blackout and then swear off it for life the next day. This resolve would last a few weeks, and then I'd have to drop into the bottle shop to speak with my local sommelier about a new wine I just 'had to experience.' I would trot home with a beautiful bottle of Shiraz from McClaren Vale or a Chianti Classico from the hills of Tuscany and get going for the night. Inevitably, that first bottle would lead to many, which usually ended with me waking up with the same sick panic attack about what had gone down the night before.

This cycle had been going on for quite some time now. So, Ash and I, both inspired by our shared love of fine Italian wine, decided to go all in and join this wine tour through the beautiful Chianti region in Italy. Picture this - rolling hills, vineyards stretching for miles, and the promise of a delicious glass of red around every bend. It sounded like heaven.

But, as we got into the tour and started tasting, something just felt off. Instead of savouring each sip of that fantastic wine or gulping it down like us, the others in the group were basically using it like mouthwash! They'd take a swig, swish it around, and then spit it out into this bucket. Can you believe it? We're in wine heaven, and they're treating it like a dentist's appointment!

Obviously, we thought it was a waste, so we decided to ditch the group, buy a few bottles, and sit at the top of the town looking over the hills and the vineyards. We high-fived each other over the stunning view and the beautiful wine, and we took photos and videos to watch back with our bored relatives and friends to show them what an amazing life we had.

Lost in the moment, I'm not sure how we found our way back to the tour bus, but when we got there, we were thoroughly smashed. I tried to befriend and overshare with half of the bus, stained purple teeth spitting all over them as they struggled to understand my drunken Aussie drawl. We ended up chatting with a photographer from Adelaide, whose ear we chewed off for the rest of the trip and who we swore we'd stay in contact with as he was our new best friend. The poor bastard probably couldn't wait to get away from us.

We dragged him along to the town square, where we again pulled out our video camera. We started filming our loud, raucousness, butting into other people's conversations, asking them to wave at the camera and say 'ciao' to my mate Sarah, my sister Debbie, or my Italian friend Michael's dad. They all obliged, but watching the footage back now, I can see how annoyed they were.

Before long, I excused myself and stumbled to the tiny toilet in which I projectile-vomited all over the walls, floor and toilet seat. Not a very classy act. I remember walking back to the hotel and feeling like the world was tipping sideways. Concerned locals gave me worried glances as Ash tried to keep me upright while I sang 'When the War Is Over' at the top of my lungs.

I can laugh about this now, but really, I'm shuddering as I write this.

It got to the point where I'd finally had enough. I was

so sick and tired of that feeling of shame and self-loathing, sick and tired of lying to myself, and I knew it was only getting worse.

I'd tried having nights where I'd only have a few drinks. Those nights would end with cups of tea and litres of water instead of projectile vomit. Those were the nights that would leave me feeling like I had my shit together. But that would often lead to complacency. I'd let my guard down, and the binge cycle would start again.

One of the greatest gifts of sobriety is not waking up with that cringe factor. Sure, I am still somewhat of an oversharer, which is probably why I have a podcast, but I can use that as a tool to show vulnerability rather than a way to try and impress people. Who was actually impressed anyway?

My confidence has soared as I've rebuilt myself and embraced the person I truly feel I was meant to be. I'm far from perfect, but I feel good about my actions. I can now say, in truth, that I'm a really great Mum, a reliable friend and worthy enough to have healthy boundaries.

While I still may not yet have an air of 'mystery,' I'm in a much happier place thanks to sobriety. I've now been alcohol-free for six years. When I first began my twelve-month journey into sobriety, I had no idea what I was doing. One thing I did know was that I was firm in my decision to quit, and I just needed a break from that anxiety-ridden girl waking up hating herself at three in the morning.

Once I'd made the decision to stop, I went at it with everything I had. I got into journaling, attended courses, wrote gratitude lists each day, and learned everything I could about self-love, compassion, addiction, genetics, neuro-linguistic programming and cognitive reframing. It all made so much sense.

I listened constantly to podcasts or read books with inspirational messages. I made sure if I had a social event, I was always stocked up with alcohol-free drinks and a time limit. I became friends with the words 'no thanks' and had a clear vision of the sober person I wanted to be.

When I look back now, I see how much I've changed. I've always been rebellious by nature, and if you told me not to do something, then that's exactly what I would go and do. I used to see getting shitfaced as a kind of rebellion, but in reality, I was actually a conformist. I was doing what was expected of me. Much as I hate to admit it, I can see now that alcohol gave me a subtle feeling of superiority over sober people, whom I saw as nerdy or boring. Now I see how short-sighted and inaccurate that was.

These days, I view sobriety as the ultimate act of rebellion, and I'm embracing this new version of the rebel that I've become.

I exercise more, eat good food and make better choices. And you know what? I'm still having a blast and feeling more connected to people than ever before. I'm genuinely proud of who I am now, and let me tell you, I absolutely live for those cosy Sunday mornings!

2.
ROAD DOG
Ash's Story

As a musician, it had never occurred to me that I should be a teetotaller. That very notion seemed to be against the spirit of music. It was only once I'd been sober for a few months that I realised just how much alcohol had been dulling my creativity for all those years.

I came from a pretty sheltered upbringing in the eastern suburbs of Melbourne. My parents had me as teenagers and were keen to give me the opportunities they never had. My Dad's side of the family are known as 'Cape Coloured people,' a mixture of the indigenous South Africans, The Khoisan people, and all of the races that combined in the burgeoning slave trade of the last four hundred years.

They came to Australia in 1972 to escape the racially oppressive apartheid, one year before the 'White Australia' policy ended. The Groenewalds came by boat and landed in the very white suburb of Croydon. Dad came from one racially oppressive country to find himself facing even more racial discrimination here in Australia.

It wasn't long before he hooked up with my blonde-haired blue-eyed Mum, much to the disappointment of the onlooking Aussie fellas, who would yell taunts like 'Get your own woman' as my Mum and Dad would walk down the street hand in hand. It became an 'us against the rest of the world' situation exacerbated by the fact that the horny little buggers got pregnant with me when mum was fifteen.

Dad was a rising star in Australian soccer, representing Australia and captaining Victoria. He came from a long line of incredible soccer players and was featured on the back of The Sun Newspaper as Australia's new Pelé.

By the time I came along, Dad was seventeen and Mum was sixteen, and the plans for Dad to play internationally came to a bit of a halt. Being so young and having a lot to prove, they were determined to bring me up right. My brother Daniel came along two years later, so with two kids before twenty, they were as strict as they were loving.

As we grew up, soccer became the family religion. We spent every weekend and most nights of the week inside soccer club rooms. Mum and Dad worked hard to put me and my other siblings who came later through private school on my dad's tradie income with one provisor. Don't fuck it up, work hard, go to uni, play soccer.

And soccer I did, until I was seventeen and broke my leg. I was out for three months and didn't receive any physio treatment, never really recovering. I was heartbroken that I had to hang my boots up at such an early age. It felt like the worst thing that could have ever happened to me, but in hindsight, it was clearly the best. I never had room to dream about a music career while pursuing sports.

I ended up getting a teacher qualification, and for a few years, I gigged four nights a week and taught full-time, thoroughly burning the candle at both ends. The whole day job thing never suited me, though. I decided to work my ass off at not having to work and eventually became a road dog. I took pride in slogging it out, but I was having the time of my life. It wasn't a job - it was the life of a musician - it was supposed to be tough. I wanted to be like my blues heroes.

When I was still in Melbourne, maybe around the

turn of the millennium, I was doing four residencies a week. One of them was as part of a duo with the talented singer-guitarist Lloyd Spiegel. He grew up a child prodigy and was a lot more experienced and professional than me at the time. Lloyd passed on the wisdom his father had laid down to him a few years earlier. It went something like, 'You don't see an accountant have a few beers and then go to work, so neither should we. Playing music is a job.'

I laughed at Lloyd's perfectly reasonable point and went and got myself a beer. I wanted to be great, but I scoffed at the idea of being professional. We were musos, not accountants!

Lloyd and I were playing a gig at The Dan O'Connell in Melbourne. The same venue where Danni had a residency with the Sweet Painted Ladies, which was her band at the time. She was delivering some posters for their upcoming gig, and we got talking during the set break.

It was funny because I noticed that I didn't move for the whole break. I was standing there, transfixed by those big blue eyes.

We hung out at the bar after the gig. It's funny, given the context of this book, but I distinctly remember her putting a beer in front of me with the explicit command, 'Drink!'

That night, we went home together, and we were inseparable from that point on. There was a hell of a lot of drinking, sex, and not turning up to our day jobs. She was from a bit more of a country-style drinking culture, where having a drink would turn into a piss-up pretty much every time. That was new to me, as I'd never had a partner like that, but I was well up for it. I loved it. There were always guitars around. I remember playing a guitar together in bed, one holding the chords, the other strumming, both sharing a cigarette.

We loved partying. We were into everything, but alcohol was the constant. We were in our early twenties, and yes, we were fools sometimes, but we were having fun.

★ ★ ★

In those early days, there was a palpable buzz in the air whenever a blues legend like Chris Wilson was slated to perform at The Dan. He was one of my heroes. It was like God himself was coming to perform. The anticipation would build as the evening wore on, and when Chris finally took to the stage, it was like the room held its breath.

I remember one particular night when he graced us with his presence. He seemed to exude an aura of greatness, a seasoned musician who knew the stage like the back of his hand.

Lloyd and I were ecstatic to have the opportunity to jam with him. As we played alongside him, I couldn't help but feel a sense of reverence for his talent and presence. Chris appeared larger than life that night, his voice booming, harmonica wailing, room shaking.

But it wasn't just his music that left an impression on me - it was his demeanour, his aura of confidence and control. Even as he enjoyed a drink or two throughout the evening, he never missed a beat, never faltered in his performance. I watched in awe as he effortlessly commanded the attention of everyone in the room.

At one point, Chris ventured behind the bar, a mischievous glint in his eye. He picked up a pint glass and filled it halfway with Bundy, then added a splash of coke for flavour. It was a moment of pure rock 'n' roll, and I couldn't help but be drawn to it. In that moment, the life of a touring musician seemed like the epitome of excitement and adventure.

As I watched Chris perform that night, I realised that I didn't want to lead a conventional life. I wanted to follow in his footsteps, to experience the thrill of the stage, the rush of performing for a crowd. And in my mind, part of that experience included indulging in the vices that seemed synonymous with the rock 'n' roll lifestyle.

Looking back now, I see how naive I was, how misguided my beliefs about the music industry were. But in that moment, all I could think about was how incredible it would be to live a life like Chris Wilson's, to be a part of something bigger than myself. And so, fuelled by a mix of youthful enthusiasm and rock 'n' roll fantasy, I embarked on my journey into the world of music, eager to see where it would take me.

After a few years on the Melbourne scene, I built up enough of a reputation to get a few albums out and start touring. To say my early touring lifestyle was gruelling is an understatement, but I loved it. I was young. I could bounce back from the hangovers and do it all again, night after night.

The average day consisted of waking up with a hangover, having an early surf and travelling down the road to the next gig. I'd have a few beers at soundcheck, a little sleep in the early evening, and then go back to the venue for a few more beers. I'd start getting tipsy or drunk before getting on stage and then drink even more beers on stage.

After the show, a few more drinks would help me wind down. Then I'd roll a joint before hitting my hotel room, and once I settled in there, I'd drink a little more and pass out. I'd then repeat this pattern for the next day, week, month and year...

Every successful band has a 'rider,' which is the listed requirements a band or artist requests for backstage. This usually consists of some food, drinks and generally shitloads of alcohol. I started my career with a few Coopers Pale Ales, followed by some green tea, but that moderate approach didn't last long. When band members and sound crew got involved, we could have three bottles of spirits, a slab of beer, and red and white wine on the rider. We'd have a solid go at it during the gig. Then, it was the tradition to go back to the hotel to get on it even harder!

I've always been a cruisy person, never making much fuss about rider-related stuff. Still, whenever I performed at a council festival or a gig outside the typical music scene, and they didn't offer an alcohol rider, I found it to be an outrage. I felt it was 'against music,' so I would stop at a bottle shop and do the right thing. I wasn't about to commit heresy. Gigging without booze felt sacrilegious!

Five or six years into my career, I was gigging endlessly around the country. I had the inspiration and influence of a band and crew to really help me get the party going every single night. I don't want to give you the impression that poor little innocent me fell into the wrong party crowd - oh no, not at all. I was leading the charge. Over time, the drinking scale went up gradually and kept going up.

When I'd go overseas, it was usually back to solo mode, but the party continued. Whenever I was on a plane, I was drinking. In the airport lounge, I was drinking the free booze. At soundcheck, I would usually have a few quiet ones and then go back to the hotel to have a nap - I was always tired. I would always get back to the gig more than an hour before I had to play. I told myself it was to warm-up, but really, I was getting my shine on.

Early in my career, taking to the stage slightly smashed felt like it helped me get into the zone, but honestly, by the time I quit, it kept me locked out of that special place.

How do I describe the zone? I guess it's different for everybody, but for me, the zone is a flow state. I refer to it as 'lift off' where you hit a sort of slightly exalted moment. There's not much thought - you're just doing it, and the music flows naturally from you. It almost feels like you're channelling. The zone is an effortless state, but the effortlessness comes from something you have to put so much focus into. You've got yourself into a state of technical competence and put the work in over a lifetime to be in that position. The zone is what you're chasing.

It's also why I got into surfing. When you're responding to what the wave does, there's no room for any of the normal monkey chatter that's in your mind 24/7. You have to be in harmony with the ocean, or you'll blow the wave and fall off. It's a level of concentration that can force you into a state of flow that's just happening naturally.

When you go for the best surf of your life, you probably only spend a couple of minutes standing on a surfboard. The rest of the time is spent paddling around, trying to catch waves. Similarly, the best gig of your life will only contain a few minutes of achieving pure lift off and sitting in that moment of sweet transcendence.

The audience can feel it when you get into that flow state, right in the zone. They lean in and start responding more. It's tangible. You will remember those moments for the rest of your life. They are the reason you keep playing music.

To me, chasing the zone is a worthy addiction. When you first start drinking, it gives you that slightly dreamy drunk state that feels like lift off. Getting loose can coax you into that thoughtless headspace a little easier. In the beginning, drinking did feel like it offered a shortcut into the zone, but over time, it stopped me from getting there.

★ ★ ★

Danni and I often discuss the irony that whatever you use alcohol for will be inverted. If you do it for confidence, in the end, it will strip you of any shred of self-respect. It's a weird equation. I drank to get on that roll and have a laugh with the audience, but in the end, I lost my spontaneity.

At the start of my career, every gig was different. I would literally make songs up on the spot. After a decade, I lost that ability. I thought it was just the audience's expectation of hearing the same favourite songs that had worn down my ability to freestyle and improvise. But, to my pleasant surprise, when I quit alcohol, I started to get that ability back!

One of my favourite things to do now is start singing about something that's going on at the gig and see if I can make it come together as a coherent song that sounds like it's always existed. Something that, at the very least, rhymes but preferably has a punchline that works. I have no idea where it's going to go. When I start going off on a tangent like that, I throw the gauntlet down to see what I can come up with under the pressure. It always works out, and every time it does, I'm just as surprised as the audience.

This is just one example of the faculties I've regained in sobriety. This one serves as a cool little yardstick for me because I remember shying away from freestyling when I was drinking because I couldn't think fast enough anymore.

Essentially, I'd lost that spark, my quick wit, my creativity. I'd hit a point where I stopped talking to the audience as much as I used to because I didn't want people to hear how drunk I was. As I jumped up on stage for a gig, I'd tell myself not to talk too much. In a sense, I knew I was below par, but I was in damage-control mode and was just getting through. I have always prided myself on loving the audience and doing my best for them, but how could I justify this?

It's so funny looking back on it now because the moment I committed to stop drinking, I didn't need a drink before I played anymore. It was that simple. I experienced so many profound changes in my career when I quit alcohol and adopted new habits and daily routines.

My midlife crisis began to turn around on the first of January 2018, when Danni and I pledged to take a year off alcohol.

It wasn't a complicated conversation. Danni told me her BFF was quitting for a year and that she'd decided to join her. I was highly critical of the idea. After a while, I kind of looked at it again and thought, 'My drinking is worse than Danni's, and if she quits, it's gonna' be a nightmare.' I rolled my eyes and said, 'Well, okay.'

I felt like it was a massive mountain to climb, but in reality, it was really just one simple decision that actually took a lot of the head work out of the equation.

I discuss this in my book Surf by Day, Jam by Night, where I interviewed some of the greatest surfer musicians of all time. Living legends and my own personal heroes like Kelly Slater, Stephanie Gilmore, Jack Johnson, Dave Rastovich and Pete Murray, to name but a few.

Drinking is firmly embedded in the stereotypical Aussie surfer's psyche. I recently had a flick through some old surf mags. There were all these images of young guys ripping in perfect waves on Indonesian boat trips, sucking down as many Bintang beers as possible. However, writing the book and interviewing these amazing people who'd been able to follow their twin passions through lengthy and distinguished careers left an indelible mark on me. It happened at a fortunate and impressionable time on my journey with sobriety.

These people are anything but trashbags.

They get up every day and continually work at making new dreams come true. That comes after living lives that most of us can only dream about. I started to see what I'd been doing wrong for the past twenty years. If I wanted to live my dreams, I'd been going about it the wrong way. What I learned from them changed me forever.

I consider myself so lucky to have shared this journey with Danni. She inspired us to start our sober journey and was there for me every step of the way as I created a new way of being for myself. She was likewise on her own uprising mission, and we supported each other through the changes.

The early days of sobriety were a special time for our family. We were still living on the Island of the Gods - Bali. I'm sure that special place played a huge part in allowing us to rebuild our lives. We discovered and developed some insanely useful techniques for not only helping us quit alcohol but also to help turn our dreams into reality.

If you do the work, you will feel amazing and start creating things you never thought possible. All this cool stuff started happening for me that I had no idea would occur when I first started on my sobriety journey.

Would much of it have happened anyway? I don't think so. My attitude was nowhere near as positive when I was drinking. I didn't have the self-belief, and I didn't have the confidence that life would conspire in my favour instead of against me.

When you're drinking heavily and experiencing a lot of hangovers, you don't have the time or focus to move toward your goals and aspirations. To be successful and happy, you need to maintain a certain level of focus and informed optimism. You must remember your purpose daily as you work towards what's important to you. When you have a hangover, all you want to manifest is some Netflix and junk food.

How you spend your days is how you spend your life. Our time on this planet is the one thing we can't buy more of. So, even if you don't think you're too badly out of control with your drinking, just having a hangover affects your ability to live the life you want. If you have hangovers regularly, that's a lot of valuable life you're chewing up there.

Everything you've accomplished so far has been despite the obstacles posed by alcohol. Take a moment to reflect on your achievements in your career, parenting, and other relationships. Now, picture how much smoother life could become if you decide to quit drinking. It has the potential to make everything easier.

The next chapter of your life is still being written. Why not make it the best one yet?

3.
IN THE FOOTSTEPS OF MY HEROES.

'I WANTED TO BE JUST LIKE MY HEROES.
BUT I DIDN'T WANT TO END UP LIKE THEM.'
ASH GRUNWALD

Ash : Robert Johnson, one of my heroes, was a master of the Delta-Blues style. Legend has it he sold his soul to the Devil at the Crossroads for his talent, but the price was an early death. You can't get bluesier than that. He died of a suspected poisoning from a jealous husband at just twenty-seven years of age. He failed to check if his whiskey bottle had been tampered with. He was in agonising pain for three days before he succumbed to his fate. For me, one of the most significant points of relevance is that he was buying and drinking entire bottles of whiskey, and that was how they rolled in those days. This was the god of my scene!

I was always shocked by the story of his death. His music changed the world, eventually morphing into rock 'n' roll. Then there's the rest of the 27 Club - Janis Joplin, Jim Morrison, Jimi Hendrix, Brian Jones, Kurt Cobain, Amy Winehouse, and the list goes on. Hendrix died choking on his own vomit after overdosing. Another legend sacrificed to the Gods of Rock.

Looking back, I realise that my musical heroes greatly impacted me more than I thought. I never separated music from drinking and partying. I wasn't even a smoker when I wasn't around music, but I couldn't rehearse or do a gig without a cigarette. They were like peaches and cream. It was almost like a religious sacrament to me. I honestly thought it was anti-music not to have alcohol mixed in and would NEVER consider sobriety. Now, reflecting on how some of my heroes died, maybe I dodged a bullet.

People were surprised when they got to know me by how much I drank. I often heard, 'Oh, you go harder than I expected. I thought you were a hippy.' I liked this on one level, but I was disappointed in myself on another. I never intended to be what people considered a big drinker. The way I saw it, I was just following a well-trodden path, so it gave me a bit of a jolt to hear that.

There were plenty of wild nights mixed in over the years, but that might not be the most dangerous part of a deeply ingrained habitual drinking pattern. The biggest dangers in a music career are boredom and tiredness. You would be shocked at how much waiting around there is as a musician. I always felt tired on the road. I just wanted to alleviate the tiredness, and the booze would give me that energy spike. It perpetuated a terrible cycle.

It's covertly dangerous. You don't see it coming. You've got hours to kill, just hanging around on site, loading in, waiting for sound checks, doing sound checks, waiting to do the gig, signing afterwards, loading out, the trip back to the hotel. It's monotonous, and you're always staring at a fridge full of ice-cold free beer.

The now sadly departed drummer of The Rolling Stones, Charlie Watts, famously said when an interviewer asked him how it felt to have played with the band for twenty-five years, 'It was playing for about five years and twenty years of hanging around.'

Before you know it, you're standing in the wings,

waiting to go on stage. You're not feeling your sharpest. Your wife is chatting away with the opening act, getting shushed by the stage manager. And you? Well, you skull a Red Bull followed by a shot, and you're on in five, four, three, two, one.

Time and time again, I made deals with myself. Only drink after the gig, only drink one before the gig, only four drinks a night, only mid-strengths, alternate water with a drink, no white wine, no brown spirits, no spirits, what a mind fuck.

Invariably, that would be too frustrating, and I could never stick to it. Moderating was just annoying. I wanted to feel the effects of the alcohol, and moderating was like half scratching an itch and impossible to stick to.

The resolve wouldn't last long, or sometimes it would, but time is long, and I gig all the time, so eventually, it'd come unstuck, and I'd be back at square one.

Over the years, the line keeps shifting. It takes more drinks to fire up, and after a while, it just doesn't work anymore. It just makes you sloppy. Your threshold is too high, so you need quite a bit of alcohol in your bloodstream to feel the effects. By the time you do feel it, you're a mess. You've gone from sober to drunk with no party in between. At least I did anyway, not the recipe for an inspired show.

And where does it end? A bottle of vodka just to get on stage?

People think that because performers are on stage, they're super confident. This is very rarely the case. Most musicians I know are introverted with loud inner critics. Is that how Hendrix was? I wonder if he felt as uncomfortable as I do schmoozing in social situations.

Some people thrive in the music industry social scene, but it makes me uncomfortable. I can't stand deliberately networking. I feel like it's not genuine.

Combine that with self-doubt, being bad with names, disliking small talk, and it's very uncomfortable. In the past, it's been a big trigger to drink.

I remember back in 2021 when I attended the funeral of Australian legend Michael Gudinski, the founder of Mushroom Records. He was a great man, and many industry insiders had gathered to mourn the loss of this legendary figure they'd been lucky to call a friend.

As the ceremony came to a close and the wake kicked off, I found myself surrounded by chatter and condolences. Names and faces blurred together in the mix, and I struggled to keep up with the flow of conversation. It felt like I was drifting in a sea of mourners, disconnected from the moment and lost in my own thoughts.

Espresso Martinis were making the rounds, tempting me with their false promises of energy and escape. Still, I'd been on my journey of sobriety for a few years at this point, so I held firm.

Back in the day, I'd have downed those martinis without a second thought, using alcohol to drown out the grief and quiet my social anxieties. But this time, I chose a different path. Instead of chasing after that temporary numbness, I opted for some much-needed shut-eye, knowing that alcohol would only lead to regret in the morning.

For those of us constantly battling our inner demons, alcohol can seem like a quick fix, offering a brief respite from grief, self-doubt and social discomfort. But it's hard to get off once we're on that rollercoaster of confidence. We ride the wave until it crashes, stranding us in a sea of regret and hangovers.

Social anxiety comes in many shapes and sizes, often leaving us feeling like a fish out of water in social situations. Small talk becomes a dreaded chore, making us nervous and unsure of ourselves, yearning for the safety of solitude. It's no wonder that for many of us, alcohol becomes the crutch we lean on in social situations.

But as I've learned through my journey, numbing grief and anxiety with alcohol only postpones the inevitable crash. It takes courage to face these strong emotions head-on, but the rewards of sobriety are worth every ounce of effort.

Danni: You know, for me, being around the 'in-crowd' always triggers my social anxiety. It's like this constant pressure to measure up, to be as cool or as accomplished as everyone else in the room. Even though people might see me as outgoing, deep down, I struggle with feelings of self-doubt and inadequacy, especially in those high-pressure situations.

It's like putting on a brave face, but inside, I'm just not feeling good enough to be there. And I know Ash feels the same way sometimes, even though we both come across as extroverts. It's like we're fighting this constant battle between our outer image and our inner doubts.

The thought of arriving at a party and being greeted by a room full of people engaged in animated conversation is overwhelming. You do your best to blend into some conversations, but you feel self-conscious and awkward.

Your palms get sweaty, your cheeks form a rosy glow, and you feel like you look nervous, which makes it worse. It makes you over-talk. Meanwhile, your inner critic is observing the scene. 'Does my breath smell? Does my butt look fat in these pants? They think I'm a dick. I'm talking about myself too much - they're all judging me and know how nervous I am. This small talk is killing me!'

At this point, you may start to panic and want to run, or you may nervously chat away with the sweat running down your back. You reach for a drink, gulp it down, and soon enough, you relax. Before you know it, the little negative critic in your mind has taken a back seat, and you're confidently chatting away.

'Wow, what was I worried about? I am the party,' you think, swag now firmly on.

As the night rolls on and the drinking continues, the shackles of inhibition are cast aside, and you're on fire. At this point you decide to switch to something stronger. That internal voice that seemed so loud is now silent. It can't get a word in edgeways anyway, as you're on the table dancing to Elton John singing loudly into an empty bottle of Moet.

'These people worship me, fuck... I can sing better than Elton John!'

Glasses clink, the music winds down, and people start to disperse, but you're still ready to go. You search through the fridge for any leftover wine and don't take the hint that the host is ready for you to go until you're standing in the driveway. Then you start texting the few friends 'that aren't boring' to see if they're up for a 'couple of drinks.'

Fast forward a few hours to three in the morning. You've woken up, your head is pounding, your mouth is dry, and you can't quite remember how you got home. You have a very slight recollection of getting into an argument with your best friend's neighbour about fuck knows what. With that memory, bang... your heart starts to pound anxiously. You desperately scramble through what happened the night before, wondering how badly you fucked up this time. You try to remember if you kept your clothes on and if your best friend is still talking to you.

'How did I do it again?' You hate yourself. You feel sick.

Your heart races as you search through your phone, looking for any evidence of who you called and for how long. You try to go back to sleep, but your heart beats like a drum in your chest. You nervously toss and turn until the sun comes up when you sheepishly send your first apology text to your BFF with a cringe emoji or a total denial.

'Great night last night. Head hurts though. You're a bad influence, Lol.'

If I blame them jokingly, we can all laugh about it, and they will text back something equally as witty, which pardons my behaviour. They were probably as bad as I was, right? I mean, we're all looking to be pardoned. You eat some Maccas on the way to work and try to ignore that shame in the pit of your stomach.

How did the person that was so nervous to talk to people at the start of the night end up so loud, such a fuckwit, all within a few hours?

Yep, you guessed it, alcohol - it's almost always the culprit.

Looking back on my past behaviours, I never truly

acknowledged my social anxiety until I conducted a podcast interview with Patrick Kennedy. As a twenty-nine-year-old living in Melbourne, Patrick shared with me his fear of small talk and how uncomfortable it makes him. Most addiction is caused by an inability to sit with our uncomfortable feelings, and a fear of small talk is one of them.

Social anxiety can be fear of social situations, fear of being judged, fear of not fitting in, fear of not knowing what to say, fear of saying too much, or fear of not saying enough. It all leads back to fear. For some, it may just be some internal chatter - for others, it could lead to a full-blown panic attack.

Gabor Maté says that we need to learn to hold our pain to heal addiction. It's in trying to escape our pain that we create our suffering. A way to escape those feelings is to drink. But jump ahead a few hours, and bam, we're caught right in the grip of full-on anxiety, feeling way worse than when we started. The very thing that we used to ease our suffering/discomfort has made us feel like hell in a handbag.

Therapist Ben Schiller recently gave a talk on social anxiety for one of our How I Quit Alcohol challenge groups. He explained that social anxiety is driven by three levels of cognition and thoughts. The first level is the feeling of needing to perform, where one has high expectations of themselves socially. The second level is conditional beliefs, such as thinking

'If I don't make some jokes, people are going to think I'm boring.'

The third level is the deepest, unconditional beliefs about oneself, such as

'I'm not enough as I am,'

which is the most common belief among people with social anxiety.

It's OKAY to make mistakes, and it's OKAY for people to see your nervousness. Remember, as a drinker, you have gotten used to masking your feelings when they don't suit you. There is actually nothing wrong with feeling social anxiety. It's completely normal, and most people feel the same way.

Ask yourself, what will happen if you feel socially anxious? Will you spontaneously combust? What's the worst that will happen if you stand back for a moment, say very little and ease your way into the conversation?

In social settings, I often remind myself, 'I feel nervous, and that's okay.'

Embracing this mindset allows me to accept myself

just as I am, without the need for alteration. It's a gentle reminder that I don't have to drown my discomfort in alcohol. Feeling a bit nervous is not only okay but also entirely natural. Instead of wishing it away, I've learned to welcome and observe it with curiosity.

Embarking on the journey to sobriety may seem daunting, but it's worth pursuing. While it may cause some discomfort, the potential for growth far outweighs the temporary unease. Embracing this discomfort is a small price to pay for the peace of mind that comes with waking up tomorrow without regrets or heightened anxiety.

During my early stages of sobriety, I adopted the practice of keeping a journal. I found it to be an indispensable tool in my personal journey towards overcoming binge drinking.

As you read this book, things will naturally come up for you, so this is the perfect time to start writing down your thoughts. You'll find that tracking your journey with sobriety will have a raft of benefits.

Quitting alcohol can, at times, feel like a walk in the park, and other times, it can feel like a real struggle. Writing can help you cope when the going gets tough.

It's so easy to slip into negative patterns and ways of thinking. Journaling keeps you honest with yourself.

Taking notes in the morning or spending just two minutes writing or reflecting each evening can be powerful anchors. This provides an opportunity to acknowledge any challenges or temptations that may arise and devise strategies to navigate them effectively.

If you really want things to shift, you've got to roll up your sleeves and dive in with an open mind. Your future can be brighter and booze-free. It's just waiting for you to claim it.

3.
THE ALCOHOL INVERSION THEORY.

'THIS BOTTLE'S GOT ME SAYING THINGS
I SHOULDN'T SAY, AND I'LL SEND OUT
MY APOLOGIES ANOTHER DAY.'

WHISKEY CREEK BY DANNI CARR

Danni : Back in our Torquay days around 2004, I was fully immersed in binge drinking mode. I was playing a lot of music, having big, boozy sessions and drinking expensive bottles of wine, which led to some pretty messy nights.

Living on the Surf Coast of Victoria was great, and we started to meet some amazing people. For years, I'd been a fan girl of a Winchelsea folk musician named Tiffany Eckhardt. I was completely obsessed with her music and deeply in awe of her songwriting.

Her music just spoke to me. They were simple tunes about her life, her relationship with fellow musician Dave Steel, the loss of her good friend, and then, later, her dad. I listened to her music constantly. I would go to her gigs and nervously talk to her at the end of the show, and she was always so lovely.

Some of my mates who lived on the Surf Coast knew her well, so we started mixing in the same circles. Dave and her were honestly the nicest, most down-to-earth people. They were at the intersection of salt of the earth and rustic cool, exactly who I wanted to be when I grew up.

One night, a mutual friend invited me to Melbourne for a dinner he was hosting. He said Tiff was coming and asked if I could give her a lift back to Torquay with us. I said yes, but I was nervous about the drive back all day. This was the moment I could hang out with her, and she would see how amazing I was and realise she wanted to be great friends with me. Vika Bull from Vika and Linda was also at the dinner, perhaps singing at the dinner (I don't quite remember). My only concern was hooking Tiffany in so that we could start our lifelong friendship.

During the car ride to the event, a buddy volunteered to be the designated driver since I was keen to enjoy a few drinks. I wasted no time and started downing my drink, so by the time we reached our destination, I was already feeling the buzz kicking in.

As the evening rolled on, the vibes were chill, and we were all having a blast. When the main course hit the table, I was pumped to dig in. I reached for what I thought was the parmesan, ready to sprinkle it over my risotto like a pro.

In my drunken state, I grabbed the container without really looking, and instead of savoury parmesan, I ended up with a shaker full of sugar.

Here I was innocently shaking sugar all over my plate, thinking I'm adding a sprinkle of cheesy goodness.

It wasn't until I took that first bite that reality smacked me in the face. The taste of sugar mixed with risotto?

Let's just say it wasn't exactly a match made in culinary heaven. I tried to play it cool, brushing off my blunder like it was no big deal, but deep down, I was cringing hard.

But that wasn't the end of my cringe-worthy escapades for the evening. Flashbacks of the car ride home come flooding back, each one more cringe-inducing than the last. There I was, in the passenger seat, my friend behind the wheel, and poor Tiffany held captive in the back.

Determined to make the most of the journey, I

decided it was the perfect opportunity to introduce Tiffany to the Tiffany mix CD I had meticulously curated for her.

As the tracks played, my wine-induced enthusiasm reached new heights, and before I knew it, I was rambling on about the significance of each song, taking her through the tracks that she was all too familiar with...as she'd written them.

Here I was, slurring with my purple, red-wine-stained teeth, explaining why each track was on the CD, what each song meant to me, why I loved it, and how it spoke to me or changed my life. With each song, I got more and more emotional.

While I was still swigging red wine in the front to keep up my bravado, I remember hand on heart crying as I sang her songs at her.

When we finally arrived at Geelong train station, Tiffany's car parked nearby, I clumsily stumbled out and in a feeble attempt to convey my gratitude and affection, I enveloped Tiffany in a hug that lingered for far too long.

But just when I thought things couldn't get any worse, fate had one final humiliation in store. With a sudden lurch, I felt the contents of my stomach rising, and before I could react, I unleashed a torrent of vomit that splattered onto Tiffany's unsuspecting shoes. It was a grand finale to an evening filled with embarrassment and regret, sealing the fate of any potential friendship that may have blossomed that night.

After that mess, the embarrassment stuck with me like glue. It wasn't just the vomit or the awkward hug - it was realising how much booze had messed me up. I was too embarrassed after that to ever go to one of her gigs again. If I crossed her path at a festival, I would have my head down sheepish, full of shame. I couldn't bring myself to face Tiffany again, couldn't bear feeling the disappointment.

But it wasn't just Tiffany I was avoiding - it was myself. Every time I thought about that night, the memories flooded back, each one hitting me with a wave of shame. I felt like I'd let her down, let myself down.

Tiffany doesn't drink and has been sober for many years. She may not even remember that night, and it may not be as big of a deal to her as it is in my head, but for me, it's one of those nights that just kills me. It became a defining moment and a constant reminder of the person I swore I'd never be again.

★ ★ ★

Since then, I've encountered countless individuals who have shared similar experiences of shame and regret stemming from their relationship with alcohol.

In my efforts to support others in breaking free from the grip of addiction, I've often found myself reflecting on what I've come to call the alcohol inversion theory.

It's a concept that underscores the paradoxical nature of alcohol's effects. It's pretty simple. Alcohol giveth and alcohol taketh away! Whatever you drink for, eventually, alcohol takes from you. It may initially provide a temporary sense of relief or confidence, but ultimately, it exacts a heavy toll, taking more than it gives.

Consider my evening with Tiffany Eckhardt as a prime example. Seeking a confidence boost, I turned to alcohol, only to find myself overwhelmed with embarrassment and shame due to my drunken antics.

Yet, as challenging as it was, this experience served as a catalyst for profound personal growth and ultimately led me to a deeper understanding of the complexities of addiction and recovery.

There's no denying that alcohol gives you something initially - otherwise, you wouldn't drink it. But when you see the equation in its entirety, the alcohol inversion theory becomes clear.

Ash : I used to believe that drinking on stage sparked my creativity and brought out my spontaneity. It seemed to work for a while, but over time, I realised it was actually draining my creative energy.

On tour, especially when fatigue set in, I'd reach for alcohol to give me a boost. Sure, it sometimes felt like I was getting a temporary burst of energy, but looking back, I can see how my performances suffered. They lacked the passion and energy that I used to bring to the stage. Instead of feeling invigorated, I'd return home from tours feeling exhausted and depleted, with little to show for it.

It's funny how I thought alcohol was giving me energy when, in reality, it was only adding to my exhaustion.

Here's a thought-provoking exercise for you - take a moment to jot down all the reasons why you turn to alcohol. Is it to inject some excitement into a gathering, to beat the boredom blues, to soothe feelings of loneliness, or to take a break from reality? Perhaps it's a way to pat yourself on the back after a tough day, to boost your confidence in social situations, to give yourself a pick-me-up, or even to ease anxiety.

Once you've got that list down, pause for a moment to reflect on the aftermath of a heavy drinking session. Consider the hangover, the remorse, and the toll it takes on both your body and your mind.

By examining alcohol's full range of effects, rather than just the fleeting pleasure of those initial sips, we gain a deeper insight into its influence on our lives.

People often turn to alcohol as a means of escaping feelings of loneliness, seeking solace in its temporary numbing effects. However, what often happens is that this reliance on alcohol leads them into a cycle of secrecy and isolation.

This pattern is all too familiar to many guests featured on the HIQA podcast, where Danni's interviews shed light on their struggles. Many people found themselves retreating further into isolation as they grappled with the need to conceal their drinking habits from loved ones. This hidden battle with alcohol only served to deepen their sense of loneliness, exacerbating the very feeling they sought to escape.

We would drink to alleviate boredom but then end

up not doing the things that lead us to a more fulfilled life, like learning something new or practising the guitar. Instead, we'd do the same things, talk on the phone to the same people, have the same conversations, watch the same music clips.

We found that from the age of twenty-five to forty, we had the same night over and over again. When you quit alcohol, you get out of a rut, which is the opposite of boredom.

This inversion theory can also be applied across your life. Alcohol may have given you good times in your twenties, but trying to replicate those same good old days as you get older can become somewhat dysfunctional and, let's face it, a little sad.

It's so important to think this through if you're seriously considering changing your relationship with alcohol. It's time to take off your rose-coloured glasses and see it for what it is. With this clarity, you can re-evaluate if it really is that good time that's sold to us on billboards.

We are never sold the reality,

'Would you like a glass of anxiety or a bottle of shame?'

This is seeing alcohol for what it really is, the

inversion of its promise.

With this newfound clarity, embracing a gratitude practice becomes not just a beneficial tool but a fundamental shift in perspective. Many of us were drinking because we thought it made us happy. However, as the inversion theory goes, we found alcohol was really making us unhappy.

A gratitude practice is one of the most unanimously accepted methods of creating genuine happiness across many faiths and modalities.

It's interesting to note that, in many cases, gratitude is simply acknowledging all the blessings already in your life. This is a mind hack because there is always something to be grateful for. The more you practise feeling gratitude, the easier it becomes to feel it.

We may have regrets from past decisions, drunken mistakes, and messy fights, but practising gratitude can help us to let go of that baggage and focus on the present.

We found that adding a gratitude component to our journal was one of the most transformative practices in early sobriety. We wrote a minimum of three things each day that we were grateful for and why. This practice unlocked new ways of observing and thinking, creating more happiness. When you're feeling grateful for your new alcohol-free life, you are less likely to begrudge the changes you're making.

Try to change it up each day, keep it fresh, and look for new things to be grateful for. When you feel there is nothing to be grateful for, get down to the most basic things - the air in your lungs, a roof over your head, and the food in your belly.

When you stop to think about it, these obvious and basic things are the most essential things in our lives - our survival depends on them. Yet we so often take them all for granted, instead focusing on the negative. In doing so, we do ourselves a huge disservice and are often blind to the everyday miracles around us.

Danni : I often find myself just taking a moment to reflect on the everyday things around the house that make life so much easier. It's like these little conveniences - they're just there, quietly doing their thing and making life smoother without us even realising it.

Have you ever stopped to think about the kettle?

It's always ready to boil up some water in a flash,

no questions asked. And then there's the washing machine, always ready to tackle those mountains of laundry like a champ.

Even something as simple as a door handle, you give it a twist, and voila! And let's not forget about the humble flushing toilet, quietly doing its job without any fuss, ensuring our daily routines go off without a hitch.

It's these small marvels of modern convenience that often go unnoticed but make such a big difference in our lives.

If you want to go to the next level in your gratitude practice, try being grateful for life's more challenging or perceived negatives. When we find the lesson to be learnt within the challenge and find acceptance and peace in what challenges us, we stop suffering from it.

What challenges you, and what can you be grateful for within that challenge?

Regardless of your current level of gratitude, it's a quality that you can successfully cultivate further. Unlike drinking, the more of it you do, the better you feel. Gratitude helps people feel more positive emotions, relish good experiences, improve their health, deal with adversity, and build strong relationships.

Gratitude not only comes with more optimism, less anxiety and depression, and greater goal attainment but also is associated with fewer symptoms of illness and anxiety, reducing our stress levels.

Make a daily list of what you're grateful for, and after a month, you will have changed your default mode of thinking. Think how long you may have been in patterns of non-gratitude and the negative impact that's had on your life.

Spending two minutes a day reflecting on happy thoughts can lower your pain, significantly improve your happiness, help you kick addictions, and completely transform you. If your mindset is strong, grateful and positive, you can deal with those little things that might throw you off track.

Writing an email or text to someone who has had a positive impact on your life is also a great way to express gratitude. It could be an old teacher who inspired you, a coach who believed in you, a friend who has always been there for you, or a colleague who has supported you at work. Letting these individuals know how much you appreciate them can strengthen your social connections and boost your overall sense of well-being. Plus, it's a wonderful way to cultivate an even deeper feeling of gratitude in your own life.

So go ahead and spread some positivity by reaching out to those who have made a difference!

5.
THE BINGE DRINKER'S TREADMILL

Ash: In 2006, I had the incredible opportunity to support the amazing Cat Empire. They were on fire, drawing crowds that could fill a small stadium with around eight thousand people at every show!

We found ourselves on some big stages, like the iconic Sidney Myer Music Bowl in Melbourne. I'll always remember this one particular solo performance there. A buddy of mine took a photo to capture the moment, and when I looked at it, I felt like a mere speck on that colossal stage.

The whole tour was like that. Every night, we stepped onto stages that seemed to stretch to infinity, and the energy from the massive crowd was electrifying. It was a time when music felt larger than life, and I was living the dream.

One night just before that Music Bowl show, Harry Angus, the co-lead singer and a great friend of mine, turns to me with his signature cheeky grin and asks,

'Are you having a few drinks tonight?'

I remember that moment clearly, the anticipation of the big show in the air.

'I'd love to, brother, but I've been trying not to drink on this tour. I'll hold off until it's over. We can have a couple of drinks together then.'

Famous last words. Little did I know that my abstinence was like an elastic band, the more disciplined I felt as a drinker the more I'd eventually... well I'll get to that.

Fast-forward to the last show of the tour in Brisbane. We were set to perform at Riverstage, and the lineup was stacked. I kicked things off, followed by The Beautiful Girls, Blue King Brown, and the grand finale, The Cat Empire.

The crowd was amazing, and my set felt electric. I left that stage relieved, stoked, and ready for a well-earned party.

After my set, I had to race into Brisbane to host a one-off special on Bluesfest that would be shown on TV. It was a collection of outstanding live performances, and all I had to do was introduce the acts. It was an honour and fun, but I was nervous as hell.

I smashed a few beers as I was driving to the studio, and as I was getting through the takes, I kept gulping the beers, noticing my nerves start to settle.

It's funny, whenever you come unstuck, you can look back and do a lot of post-fuck-up-forensics. You see that it's usually caused by a rare combination of factors. In this case, I was always destined to get blind because it was the last show of the tour, and I'd been abstaining all this time. But suppose you throw an unusual situation that makes you nervous or excited into the equation. Then you're looking at a killer combo.

I returned to Riverstage in time to watch The Cat Empire preside over thousands of screaming fans. As the music pulsed through the air and the crowd roared with excitement, I found myself swept up in the electrifying energy of the concert. They were in their element, commanding the stage with effortless charisma as thousands of people danced and sang along to their every beat.

With another drink in hand, I watched from the sidelines, soaking in the atmosphere and revelling in the joyous chaos around me.

When the boys finally finished their set, the backstage area erupted into a frenzy of celebration. We clinked glasses and toasted to our shared success, the cheers and laughter echoing through the night air.

Considering that I was already at least six drinks in when they got off stage, and they were just starting, I decided to leave the hire car behind at the venue.

With a slight wobble in my step, I made my way to the commuter van with the rest of the band. But as luck would have it, there were no available seats left, leaving me with little choice but to claim a spot on the floor. So, there I was, sprawled out amidst a sea of legs, chatting away with the guys as we made our way to some random pub.

As the van rumbled down the darkened streets, I couldn't help but laugh at the surrealness of the moment. Here I was, living out my rock 'n' roll fantasy. I'd just finished up one of the best tours of my career. I was surrounded by music and friends I admired, and I was completely lost in the thrill of the night. Little did I know, the evening was only just beginning.

I had this habit of getting into these cocktail and spirit fads back then. I'd get fanatical and then move on to the next very strong drink. It never occurred to me that maybe I was more into getting fucked up than the specifics of the flavours and aromas I could be found pontificating about.

At this particular moment, I was all about a drink called a Rusty Nail, made from Drambuie and scotch. It's not the sort of thing the casual drinker swills while already dehydrated on a balmy Brisbane night.

My main memory from the pub is me screaming, 'Salvadore! Roll a joint!' across the bar.

I even remember shouting a couple of Rusty Nails for Harry and Felix, and my voice was booming across the place. Looking back now, as someone who is generally quiet and mellow offstage, I want to hide under a rock. When I think about these moments of being loud and obnoxious, it makes me cringe.

You see, I've got a pretty sizable head, a wide mouth, and a barrel chest. That's why I've got a booming singing voice, but when I've had a couple, I can be downright annoying without even realising it.

During my U.S. tour with Xavier Rudd, it seemed like every night was a party. For six weeks straight, I had a drink in hand, following the same routine - sign CDs, down tequila and beer, and convince myself I was just chatting away. But looking back, I was probably shouting my head off by midnight.

One morning, after a particularly wild night, I decided to join Xav for a run. As we jogged along, he turned to me with that classic Aussie sincerity and said something like,

'Mate, it's all good to let loose after the gig, but your voice just gets so damn loud!'

It was a wake-up call, to say the least. Here I was, thinking I was just having a good time, but in reality, my behaviour was affecting those around me.

That moment stuck with me, highlighting one of the peculiarities of alcohol - its ability to impact each of us differently. Alcohol has this funny way of magnifying our quirks, and for me, it meant turning up the volume a few notches too high.

★ ★ ★

Alright, let's rewind a bit. So, there I was, back at the pub, fully embracing party mode. I was hollering across the bar for that joint and another round of Rusty Nails, feeling like I was on top of the world. But little did I know, that was the last clear memory I'd have for the night before I entered the dreaded blackout zone.

The next thing I knew, I was snapping back to reality in a dingy alley behind the pub, my head pounding like a drum and my mouth drier than the Sahara. The combination of all-day drinking, those lethal Rusty Nails, the sweltering heat, and the lack of hydration hit me hard.

I remember thinking as I was half-passed out, 'You know what? I'm okay here.'

Harry or someone from the Cat Empire offered to take me somewhere, but I declined. I couldn't even remember where my hotel was, and that warmth felt kind of nice.

But then Pete Wilkins, the drummer from Blue King Brown (who would later tour and record with me on the Now album), stepped in and insisted I join them. He helped me back to their place and tossed me into one of the spare beds.

The next morning, the hangover hit me like a freight train, right in the sweltering Brisbane heat. Somehow, I managed to get a taxi to my car, drove to the airport, and hopped on a plane. I'd never felt so dreadful in my life. By the time I landed back in Melbourne, I was an absolute mess.

I rushed to the toilet, vomited, and then, as I went back for my bags, I had to dart back to the bathroom again. This routine continued until the hangover started playing tricks on me.

I'd head for my bag, feel the need to run back to the toilet, only to return without hurling. This went on for a bit, and then it happened. Right when I was furthest from the toilet, I couldn't hold it in any longer. I puffed out my cheeks, and it sprayed out horizontally. Embarrassed, I ran away from the scene, cleaned myself up, and finally grabbed my bags.

Danni, bless her soul, was the one picking me up from the airport that day. As soon as she saw me stumbling out, reeking of last night's booze, she couldn't hold back.

'Why did you get so wasted?' she asked, her tone a mix of concern and disbelief.

So, there I was, barely able to stand, covered in specks of vomit, but I knew I had to spill the beans. I told her everything that had gone down the night before, the wild partying, the blackout before waking up in the alleyway. And just when I thought things couldn't get any crazier, Danni dropped a bombshell of her own.

'Well, you won't like this, but I'm pregnant!' she announced, her eyes wide with shock.

And just like that, in the midst of my hangover haze, I found out we were expecting our first child, Sunny. It was like a lightning bolt to the brain, a wake-up call ringing loud and clear. But the big question remained - did I actually pay attention to it?

Despite my honest attempts, the journey towards change was far from smooth sailing. Time and time again, I found myself falling back into old habits despite my best intentions. It seemed like my subconscious was determined to cling to its familiar comfort zone, even when it was clear that change was vital for my well-being and the future of our expanding family.

When our efforts to change fall short, it's easy to point fingers or make excuses. But the truth is, it's not about blame - it's about our subconscious, happily cruising on autopilot. It loves its comfort zone and will fight tooth and nail to stay there, even if it's doing us more harm than good.

When we act from our conscious mind, we make conscious decisions and use our willpower to elicit change. However, it takes a lot of effort to stay in the conscious mind, and our subconscious wants the old patterns back. So how do we change?

We have to educate our subconscious mind and teach it to change through repetition, daily practice, daily journaling, and challenging our old thought patterns.

As Dr. Wayne Dyer says,

'Progress and growth are impossible if you always

do things the way you've always done things.'

If you think the same thoughts, you will have the same emotions. If you have the same emotions, you will take the same actions, and if you take the same actions, you will have the same outcomes.

We want to create new outcomes by disrupting the old way of thinking, the old patterns and behaviours.

The first step is becoming consciously aware. This is not always easy, but when you can become aware of your negative patterns, try to challenge them. Do something different, choose a different thought, even laugh at the old familiar voice saying the same familiar thing.

When that voice gets in your ear and tells you that it's okay to have just one drink. Laugh at it! Say,

'I know what you're up to, and you won't fool me again.'

Each time you challenge it and win, you create new neural pathways, making it easier and easier next time.

When you take personal responsibility for the way you feel and act, you take control of your life rather than leaving it up to the whims of your external environment, which, as we know, can change at any point.

When you observe your thoughts, you can question the validity of them, just like your limiting self-beliefs.

Often, we believe things about ourselves or our circumstances to be accurate but don't question the evidence we have to support those beliefs. See your beliefs as a tabletop and the evidence that supports those beliefs as the legs. If you knock out the legs from under the table, there is nothing to hold it up, and it collapses. You create doubt by looking at the evidence in a different way.

You can use this same method to create new, more positive beliefs about yourself. You need to have your own back, as no one else can do this for you. Luckily, our brains have great neuroplasticity, and even if your heart isn't 100% into it, this hack works. You can begin a gentle rewrite of your story by practising it, and you can use this with all thoughts you have about alcohol or any limiting belief you have about your life.

If you're struggling to believe you can change, remember a time in your life when you felt confident or achieved something you didn't think you could. Even if that thing was way back in childhood.

Maybe it was scoring a goal in your favourite sport, cooking something wonderful, training a pet to do a trick, or helping someone.

We all have something we thought we couldn't do, and we managed to do it. And this challenge is exactly the same.

You have it in you.

You can change.

You just have to make the choice.

You always have a choice.

You choose if you're going to put a drink to your lips, you choose if you're going to hit the fuck-it button, or you choose to sit with your feelings and make it through this.

You CAN do it.

6.
EXCUSES, EXCUSES

Your mind is an expert architect of excuses, especially when it comes to alcohol. It's like a skilled craftsman meticulously constructing a labyrinth of justifications to lure you back to the bottle.

'Just one won't hurt,'
it whispers seductively while simultaneously painting a vivid picture of relaxation and enjoyment.

With each excuse carefully crafted and seamlessly presented, it's easy to get trapped in a tangled web of rationalisations.

That's exactly why we've taken the time to gather and dissect the most common excuses people give for drinking.

We're here to shine a light on each one, revealing why they are utter bullshit and are instead just flimsy justifications for harmful behaviour. Let's start with the most common one.

'I love having a drink. Alcohol is my buddy.'

Imagine if I shared with you that every time I hung out with this friend, I woke up with shame, embarrassment, remorse, anxiety, headaches, and lethargy, what would you advise me to do with that friendship?

Run for the fucking hills, that's what.

Is alcohol really treating you the way you would want a friend to treat you? Would your friends make you feel depressed and sick? Would your friends egg you on to keep travelling further into a life-threatening rabbit hole of disease and possible addiction? Life is hard enough without friends that fuck you up.

'But it relaxes me.'

How relaxed do you really feel at three in the morning when you wake up with deep regret? Your sympathetic nervous system is hitching a ride on the booze train, picking up steam, shedding inhibitions, and hurtling toward a morning of wreckage.

Ethanol throws your mind into chaos on every front. Sure, you might feel relaxed at first, but after a few drinks, you're anything but relaxed. Instead, you're embarking on a rollercoaster of adrenaline spikes and hormonal chaos that can take days for your body to rebalance.

'Nothing beats a cold beer on a scorching Aussie summer day.'

Basking in the sun with a drink in hand feels like an essential part of the Aussie experience - whether it's at the beach, the cricket, or just chilling out in the backyard.

It's easy to see it as a refreshing treat, a reward for enduring the heat. But let's cut through the nostalgia and get real for a moment.

For those of us who tend to overindulge, what starts as a polite sip can quickly spiral into a full-blown bender. So, before you crack open that next cold one, ask yourself - can you really stop after just a couple? Or will those 'can't stop' cravings kick in, leading you down a path you'd rather avoid?

Think about it - day drinking might give you a buzz in the afternoon sun, but it often morphs into a messy night ahead. And trust me, nobody wants to end up like those dishevelled partygoers stumbling out of the Melbourne Cup, swapping their glamour for vomit-stained chaos.

'It gives me confidence.'

But how confident do you feel when you're flashing back to the night before, where you spent all evening cracking onto your neighbour's spouse, sparking an argument that escalated until dawn?

When you wake up with a sick hangover and raging hangxiety, the initial burst of alcohol-fuelled confidence inevitably fades into a dopamine and serotonin low tide.

That sick, anxious dread can last for days. Remember the alcohol inversion theory - what the alcohol promises is actually what it's taking away from you. Alcohol is destroying your confidence and self-esteem.

'It's my reward.'

But how rewarding is forgetting the supposedly good time you had, only to wake up in a shit storm of day-after self-loathing? How rewarding is it to feel physically sick with the sting of vomit in your throat? This excuse is one of the hardest to ignore.

We've been conditioned by cultural norms and the media at large to believe that alcohol is a reward.

For some, the reward is sitting down with a glass of wine at the end of the workday or after putting the kids to bed. It's permission to turn off, relax, and enjoy. You feel like you deserve it.

We all like a reward, but can you find another way? Can you create a reward system that doesn't leave you with shame, regret, and anxiety?

Do you really need ethanol poisoning, carcinogenic chemicals, and an estrogen dump to reward yourself?

These things are the opposite of a reward - in a way, they're a punishment. The initial feeling of reward is fleeting, and then you're left feeling sour and with a crushing hangover.

You can find other ways to treat yourself, like making an extra special mocktail that you can indulge in as much as you want. This is so much better than drinking alcohol and damaging your health. Your improved health is the best reward.

'But my friends won't like me. People will think I'm boring.'

How interesting are you when you repeat yourself,

talk over everyone, and tell the same old stories? Hanging around people who are getting smashed might start to feel a bit stale when you're sober. You might come to realise that instead of you being boring, they're the ones who are actually boring to you.

The friends you fear will dislike you for quitting are probably drinkers themselves. If someone genuinely dislikes you when you're sober and encourages you to drink, well, we hate to break it to you, but they're an 'enabler.'

Enablers want everyone to be on their level, stuck in a cycle of overindulgence and regret. It somehow eases their burden to have company in their reckless behaviour. So, enablers are driven by their own issues or addictions, not by concern for your well-being.

If you end up more messed up on alcohol than they are, they'll likely feel a twisted sense of satisfaction, thinking, 'Well, at least I'm not that bad,' or 'At least I'm not the only one.' And if everyone is intoxicated together, then no one remembers anything the next day, so who cares, right? There's safety in a collective blackout, as if your regrettable behaviour doesn't count if no one remembers it.

Your real friends will cheer for your choice to

prioritise your well-being and happiness over a night of heavy drinking.

Don't internalise the enabler's projections that you're now dull or less cool. The reality? You're anything but boring - it's actually the drinkers who might be lacking in excitement. Let's face it, intoxicated people might crack jokes or voice their opinions loudly, but they're not always as witty or entertaining as they believe.

'I'll lose my edge.'

How edgy do you feel when you're slowly morphing into just another run-of-the-mill dimwit? The act of being drunk doesn't make you unique. You're just like everyone else, and any old dickhead can get drunk.

You might think you're sophisticated, but as you drink more, you descend into a place where the finesse of your personality fades away. You're more unique, authentic, and edgy when you're sober.

This excuse holds significant sway in the arts industries, where there's a long-standing tradition of glorifying those who've succumbed to the allure of drugs and alcohol. However, the music business, for example, has evolved since the wild days of the 1970s.

It's now populated by focused and dedicated

individuals, and the glamour of excess is losing its appeal. Your edge, what you might consider 'cool,' is at stake. Is it cool to get sloppy and loud, lose control, stumble, and vomit on your friend's shoes?

Is it cool to deliver less than your best performance? Is it cool to look tired, red-faced, and bloated? The reality is that quitting alcohol sharpens your edge. This is one of the most remarkable benefits for any musician or performer.

'I use it to cope.'

But does getting drunk ever change your situation for the better? Your dog died. You get plastered. You wake up with a hangover. The dog is still dead. Now, on top of grieving, you have to make apologetic phone calls. How's that for coping?

And here we are. This is where the healing begins. You're relying on a substance, thinking it's your lifeline, but it's not. You believe it eases your pain, but in reality, it's just a band-aid on a big, wobbly mess.

The truth is, alcohol isn't helping you cope - it's enabling you to avoid reality. The more you drink, the more out of control things become. Drinking alone or hiding it from others should be red flags.

Alcohol doesn't help you cope. It amplifies the chaos and repetitive cycles of addiction. We all encounter problems, trials, and pain. They're an inevitable part of life, a guaranteed degree of suffering.

Whether you're wealthy or struggling, problems will arise, causing anxiety and discomfort. Nobody enjoys pain, and it's natural to seek relief from it. But using alcohol as a Band-Aid for discomfort provides only temporary relief.

If you've been using alcohol to numb your pain, it's time to confront the skeletons lurking in your closet. It takes courage to shed old skin, take accountability, and practice radical self-love.

These skeletons, hidden for too long, have influenced your subconscious reactions and weighed you down with baggage. They may not want to be found, but their presence affects your decisions and patterns, hindering your ability to thrive. It's time to release them and lighten your load.

★ ★ ★

Facing your emotions with gentle inquiry and compassion is the first step on this journey.

It's tough when you start realising that you might be edging towards a boundary with your alcohol consumption.

This realisation can be jolting, confronting, and downright scary. Feelings of dismay and shame may wash over you, especially if you've been in denial about the extent of the issue. The stigma attached to being labelled a problem drinker can be difficult to grapple with.

Even if you're not physically addicted to alcohol, habitual excessive drinking can create a psychological dependency.

Quitting alcohol demands unwavering focus and dedication. For some, it feels like a complete identity shift, leaving them uncertain of who they are without the booze.

We've experienced this firsthand. It's like embarking on a journey of self-discovery all over again, bidding farewell to the drunken life we once knew.

It takes courage and strength to confront your demons and work through your struggles. But facing your challenges head-on is the path to true liberation and growth.

Give it a shot, and try not drinking for just one evening. Take note of the behaviours of any heavy drinkers around you. It's not about passing judgment

- it's about simply observing.

As you witness the actions of others under the influence, you might start recognising some familiar patterns. You might notice their lack of inhibitions, impaired judgment, and the potential for drama or risky decisions lurking around the corner of their next drink.

These moments of observation can serve as a wake-up call, highlighting the potential consequences of heavy drinking. As you witness the behaviour of others under the influence, it prompts reflection on your own drinking habits and the triggers that lead you down a similar path.

It's a chance to take stock of where you're headed and consider whether you want to continue down that road. Rather than feeling judgmental, it's an opportunity for self-awareness and recognition of the patterns that may be holding you back from living your best life.

We've all used the above excuses to justify our drinking habits. By acknowledging these excuses, we take the first step towards regaining control over our lives and making healthier decisions.

It's not about assigning blame or feeling guilty, but

about embracing honesty and courage as we navigate towards a more fulfilling and authentic path.

Each excuse we kick to the curb is a chance to level up. With some grit and a little help from our friends, we can rewrite our stories and carve out a future that's all about seeing things clearly, living with purpose, and finding our happy groove.

7.
CONFESSIONS OF AN INSTIGATOR

Danni: About two years into my sobriety, I got invited to a good friend's birthday dinner. She runs in circles with what people might call the 'in' crowd.

As I've spoken about in previous chapters, the whole 'in' crowd thing has always made me feel a bit uneasy as an adult.

Most of us can relate to that feeling of not quite fitting in, not feeling cool enough, pretty enough, or not measuring up in some way.

I was seriously considering backing out. I mean, the thought of it was enough to send shivers down my spine. A local restaurant, crowded with people I sort of knew but didn't really feel comfortable around? That was basically my idea of hell.

But after going through multiple wardrobe changes and giving myself a few motivational speeches in front of the mirror, I finally mustered up the courage to head over to Saint Maries in Brunswick Heads. It was one of those places teeming with hipsters and stunning individuals, which only added to my nerves.

Approaching the table, I was met with a sight straight out of a bohemian dream - ten women, all in their late thirties to early forties, adorned in ethereal Spell dresses.

They looked effortlessly chic, and here I was, feeling like a fish out of water.

My nerves kicked into high gear as I approached. Suddenly, I became acutely aware of my own self-consciousness.

My heart was pounding so loudly that I was sure they could hear it. And was my face turning red? I couldn't shake the feeling that my hair was starting to frizz up in the humidity, adding yet another layer of insecurity to the mix.

As I tentatively made my way around the table, exchanging greetings and kissing cheeks, I couldn't shake the feeling of nervousness creeping into my voice. Taking a moment to survey the scene, I noticed the unmistakable presence of red wine in the hands of each woman gathered around the table. At the same time, a half-full carafe rested at the table's centre, accompanied by glasses of sparkling water.

I squeeze into a seat beside the most familiar face and make the dreaded small talk.

Part of me secretly hopes they'll all get so drunk and be too engrossed in their own conversations to notice my anxious fidgeting.

I find myself speaking in hushed tones, almost as if I'm attempting to conceal any traces of self-doubt. Amidst it all, I can't shake the nagging worry about my breath, so I resort to speaking softly, almost as if I'm breathing inwards to mask any potential odour.

I feel like they're silently judging my appearance and thinking I'm not quite up to their standard. Maybe they're thinking that my skin isn't perfect, or my hair is too bright. The urge to bolt back home hits me like a ton of bricks, but I take a moment to gather myself and just observe what's going on.

Just then, another friend breezes in. She's the girlfriend of a local musician, another beautiful person who oozes laid-back charm. She's captivating like the others, but there's something real about her that instantly relaxes me. With her quick wit and playful banter, she effortlessly cuts through the tension, melting away the awkwardness.

As she playfully comments on the irony of me being sober here, a memory flashes in my mind. I remember the last time we hung out, back at my place, laughing and joking over drinks.

It was supposed to be a casual lunch on my deck with just a few friends, but things quickly escalated. Before we knew it, we'd polished off about six bottles of Champagne, and someone had the bright idea to call up the local dealer for a bag of coke.

As the day turned into night, we found ourselves snorting lines, downing drinks, and eventually making our way down to the beach for a spontaneous skinny dip.

I don't even know how they got home, as I must have passed out before they left.

I remember waking up the next day feeling like death. I was shaking and anxious and pretty much wanted to die. I begged Ash to get the kids off to school and stayed curled up in the foetal position for half the day.

How did this happen again, and with a couple of

friends who are fairly quiet types?

I seem to do it all the time, invite people over who don't drink a lot and try to get them as fucked up as possible, all in the name of a good time, getting to know them better or loosening them up a bit.

But looking back, I think it was because I felt a little uncomfortable or like I wasn't quite 'enough' for those particular people.

It would usually be people who were famous musicians, intelligent, super cool, or super beautiful. All the things that brought out my own insecurities.

I didn't know how to feel at ease, so I would get wasted and take them down with me. Of course, I did this with familiar friends as well, but it seemed to go a step further with people I half knew.

As the night wore on in Brunswick Heads, I observed the women around me nursing their glasses of red wine, their laughter and conversation filling the air. Gradually, I began to relax and engage more in the lively chatter. When the pizzas arrived, we eagerly dug in.

I noticed their glasses gradually emptying.

Eventually, the waiter approached our table, inquiring if they would like another round of drinks or perhaps another bottle of wine to keep the festivities going.

As I watched them, I was waiting for that glint in their eyes, you know?

Like, the 'Fuck yeah, let's keep this night rolling' kind of vibe, or maybe just a laid-back 'Why not, right?'

But instead, they all passed on more wine and opted for sparkling water. I couldn't believe what I was witnessing!

A few of the ladies snuck off for a sneaky rollie, and the rest of us posed for a few Instagram selfies. Then, after a bit more chit-chat, I said my goodbyes and headed out, still processing what had just happened.

When I got home, I woke Ash up to tell him what I'd witnessed. How none of them even bothered with a second drink, let alone another bottle. It really struck me just how differently the night might've played out if I'd been drinking too.

I would have conned at least one of them into having another bottle or three. We would have got someone to drive us back, or perhaps I would have driven (because it's only around the corner) and then continued at my place.

Ash and the kids would've been subjected to the chaos of Elton John blasting through the house on an otherwise quiet Wednesday night. They would have had to endure the sounds of us loudly singing before dragging Ash out of bed, insisting he join us in our antics.

Once Ash was reluctantly pulled into the mix, there would have been no escaping our shenanigans. He would've been lured into our mischievous plans, whether he liked it or not. The evening would have transformed into a whirlwind of laughter, music, and questionable decisions.

But thankfully, sobriety prevailed, sparing Ash and the kids from the uproar of a midweek party. And for that, we were all grateful.

This was a big moment for me. Even though I was a couple of years into my sobriety, I had never stopped to realise what an enabler I was.

I would drag other people into my shit show, and it all stemmed from my own insecurities and not (as I thought) because I wanted them to have a good time. I didn't want them to notice my inadequacies.

I was the instigator.

Recognising the significant role that insecurities played in shaping my life was a wake-up call. It spurred me to embark on a journey of cultivating self-love, a practice that would prove to be transformative.

We naturally gravitate towards healthier decisions when we genuinely love and accept ourselves. Why would we subject ourselves to substances that harm us when we're in a place of complete self-acceptance?

For too long, we've internalised negative beliefs, convincing ourselves of our inadequacies and unworthiness. So how do we start to love ourselves more?

It begins with a simple shift in perception, a decision to see ourselves through a lens of acceptance and appreciation.

Instead of pointing out every flaw, let's celebrate our uniqueness and individuality. After all, it's our quirks and idiosyncrasies that make us beautifully human.

Let's replace self-criticism with self-compassion, offering ourselves the same level of understanding and support that we would readily extend to a friend in need.

When faced with setbacks or challenges, let's respond with gentle encouragement rather than harsh judgment.

Embracing ourselves just as we are doesn't mean stagnation or complacency. It's about acknowledging our inherent worthiness and recognising that we are deserving of love and respect, regardless of our perceived shortcomings.

Start by standing in front of a mirror and connecting with yourself on a deeper level. Look into your eyes and affirm, 'I love you. I really, really love you.' While it may feel uncomfortable initially, this act of self-affirmation gradually becomes a powerful gesture of self-love and care.

Another beautiful practice is to release the burden of worrying about others' opinions and focus on what truly resonates with our authentic selves. When that inner critic starts to chime in, let's gently challenge those negative thoughts and replace them with positive affirmations.

By writing them down, repeating them in our minds, and speaking them aloud, we set the stage for a more empowering self-narrative. Remember, the words we choose to follow, 'I am,' shape our reality, so let's ensure they reflect our worth and potential.

Start each day by taking a moment to recognise yourself for simply being who you are. Whether it's getting out of bed with a smile or tackling a challenging task head-on, every little accomplishment counts. Acknowledge and celebrate your victories, no matter how small they may seem. This celebration is key to building up your self-esteem and resilience.

As you go about your day, don't forget to pat yourself on the back for the positive choices you make. It might even be choosing something healthy over fast food or taking a moment to breathe during a stressful situation, each decision deserves acknowledgment.

Instead of dwelling on perceived failures or shortcomings, shower yourself with praise. By adopting a mindset of self-compassion and celebration, you create a nurturing environment for growth and self-discovery. So go ahead, give yourself a round of applause - you deserve it!

Finally, give yourself the incredible gift of forgiveness. Take a moment to grab a pen and paper, and jot down any lingering feelings of guilt or regret. Then, follow each statement with 'I forgive myself for.'

It might feel a bit awkward at first, but trust me, it's worth it. This practice of self-forgiveness is like planting seeds of healing and growth within yourself. It takes time, but each act of forgiveness is a step forward towards greater clarity and self-compassion.

So go ahead, let those words flow onto the page. Forgive yourself for the mistakes you've made, the opportunities you've missed, and the times you've fallen short. With each forgiveness, you're making space for new beginnings and a brighter future.

Keep in mind that true change starts from the inside out.

When you fully embrace yourself, every flaw, every quirk. You open the door to incredible transformation and growth.

Make a pledge to cultivate a gentler, more loving relationship with yourself. Understand that this journey isn't about reaching some ideal of perfection - it's about making strides, no matter how small, toward becoming the best version of yourself.

So, take a deep breath, trust in the process, and embrace the beauty of your imperfectly perfect self. This is where your journey truly begins.

8.
THE THIEF & THE BROTHEL

Ash : A few years back, I attended a friend's wedding at a local venue in Newcastle called Lizotte's. The crowd was an eclectic mix of personalities, including one of Australia's biggest hip-hop acts. Spirits were high, elevated by copious drinks and perhaps a few 'lines' here or there.

The groom had been my sound guy for many years. We toured the country together countless times and had some fun post-gig escapades. One of our most cherished rituals was our late-night downhill skateboarding sessions, fuelled by a mix of alcohol and adrenaline. It became our version of a sacred tradition, a ritual that we eagerly looked forward to after each successful show.

The reception started to get wild, fermenting into rock'n'roll festival debauchery. All parties dug in and began to charge hard. Caught up in the frenzy, I felt myself spiralling out of control, swept away by the night's energy.

It was a familiar sensation, one I'd stumbled into too many times - a plunge into intoxication where all sense of restraint was abandoned, and recklessness reigned supreme.

As time slipped by, a sinking feeling gnawed at my gut. I couldn't ignore the truth. I'd become that loud, annoying guy I couldn't stand. Yet, amidst the turmoil and shame, there was a strange comfort in the chaos.

Amidst the madness, I wrestled with conflicting emotions - embarrassment mixed with a strange sense of freedom. It was a messy cocktail of self-disgust and indulgence.

A cover band was playing, and I somehow ended up on stage. I can't remember if I was invited, but apparently, I was on fire. Now, I'm not exactly known for my dancing skills. In fact, I'm more at home strumming a guitar than busting a move. But there I was, channelling the spirit of James Brown, Fred Astaire, and 'Plugger' (the legendary AFL full forward) all rolled into one.

I couldn't say if I was hitting all the right notes or tripping over my own two feet, but from what I gathered, Danni seemed impressed. Still, as the memories of that wild night flood back, there's a tiny voice in the back of my mind whispering, 'I hope there's no footage!'

Before I knew it, the night had crept into the early hours, and we found ourselves holed up in a cosy little bar, drinks in hand. But there was a hitch - the bar had closed its doors for the night. Amidst the dimly lit ambience, the groom's hand found its way to my shoulder, a gentle yet firm gesture that spoke volumes.

'Grunny, take a seat,' he urged, his tone more concerned than angry.

Confusion clouded my mind as I tried to piece together the events of the evening.

'What happened?' I asked, genuinely confused by the turn of events.

As the details began to surface, a sinking feeling settled in the pit of my stomach. Apparently, entirely out of the blue, I'd started hurling insults at the bartender in a manner that was completely uncharacteristic of me.

'Give us a drink, ya fat cunt!'

The words echoed in my mind, spoken with a volume and fervour that was so out of character.

But here's the kicker - I wasn't there. Or at least, my consciousness wasn't present for the spectacle. It was as if I had been a mere spectator to my own actions, watching in shock and disbelief as the scene unfolded before me.

In that moment, I was as stunned as everyone else, grappling with the unsettling realisation that I was capable of such outbursts, even in a state of drunkenness. It was a sobering reminder of the unpredictable nature of alcohol and its ability to strip away our inhibitions, revealing a side of ourselves we barely recognise.

We staggered off into the night, exhaustion weighing heavy on our shoulders, until we finally reached the hotel. There, parked out front, stood our touring motorhome, as one of our bandmates would be staying in there. But something was off - the giant toolbox bolted to the back was wide open, our precious gear, or what was left of it exposed to the crisp Novocastrian breeze.

Shock coursed through me as we frantically dialled the police, our hearts sinking with each passing moment. As we paced nervously, waiting for help to arrive, someone mentioned seeing a man across the street, casually strumming a Cole Clark acoustic guitar - a guitar that looked suspiciously like one of ours.

In a surge of adrenaline, I felt myself swell with anger,

my instincts urging me to confront the thief. Danni remembers how I puffed up, my chest swelling like a silverback gorilla, as I marched across the street with purpose. She feared I would resort to violence, a side of me she had never seen before. But in that moment, I was fuelled by a righteous indignation, determined to reclaim what was rightfully ours.

I stormed over, propelled by a potent mix of anger and frustration, and snatched the guitar from his grasp.

'What the fuck do you think you're doing?' I yelled, my voice thick with rage, as I shoved him around aggressively.

I don't recall much about the guy except that he was small, wiry, and utterly unfazed by my outburst.

Despite my threats and blustering, he remained calm and collected, almost nonchalant in the face of my fury. It was as if he had expected this confrontation and was prepared to weather the storm.

In that moment, I realised that my attempts at intimidation were futile, like trying to tame a wildfire with a water pistol.

He appeared bewildered as he attempted to justify his actions, saying,

'I just needed some cash to busk, you know, so I could head inside and get one of the ladies.'

It was then that I noticed he was standing right outside a brothel, adding another layer of absurdity to the situation.

As the police arrived, I launched into a passionate retelling of the events, my voice escalating to a crescendo of frustration as I berated the guy once more. I could feel my anger rising, my words coming out in a torrent of screams and profanities.

By then the officers had started to chuckle, their laughter cutting through the tension like a refreshing breeze. It was like they'd tossed a bucket of water on my fiery anger, instantly giving me a dose of perspective on the whole situation.

Looking back, it was just one of those crazy nights where everything seemed to spiral out of control. That feeling of coming to your senses briefly in the middle of some crazy situation and then falling back into the maelstrom as the substance takes the wheel back is so wild.

There were many other nights like that, as I'm sure many of you can relate.

There's something that I like about the chaos.

There's a certain allure to it, isn't there? It's like a magnetic force that pulls us in, even as we know it's probably not the best idea.

Maybe it's the rush of adrenaline, the thrill of not knowing what's going to happen next, or perhaps it's the feeling of freedom that comes from throwing caution to the wind.

But let's be real, chaos has its downsides too. It's unpredictable, it's overwhelming, and it can leave us feeling completely lost in the madness. In the midst of chaos, it's easy to forget who we are and what we stand for.

Still, there's something oddly satisfying about escaping chaos's clutches. Stepping back from the edge, regaining control over our lives. It's like finding peace in the midst of a storm.

I may not fully understand my fascination with chaos, but I'm grateful for the moments of clarity that come when it's finally over.

In those moments, I can't help but feel a sense of relief and gratitude for the peace that follows in its wake.

I feel much more relaxed now, knowing that no situation will ever take that weird turn. It was always so uncomfortable towards the end. Turning up to a great party or an important social situation, hoping to god that I wouldn't go too far but knowing deep down that it was up to the gods.

Maybe I'd keep it together, or maybe I'd get caught up in the moment. It's a weird situation. Let's have a good time but somehow not have too much of a good time. Pretty hard to do for a self-confessed fun junkie.

★ ★ ★

That's where the 'it's easy' technique came in handy during my first year of sobriety. This was a simple yet powerful mindset shift that completely transformed my outlook.

It all began a few weeks into my sobriety during an Aussie rock event headlined by Jimmy Barnes. As the riders were being sorted, I overheard my sound guy, Mugga, responding to a query about my preferences.

'Oh, Ash doesn't drink,' he casually remarked.

That simple statement struck me like a bolt of clarity. Until then, I'd been crafting elaborate explanations each time I declined alcohol, feeling the need to justify my choice. But in that moment, I realised it was easy.

I just had to say, 'I don't drink.'

The person Mugga was talking to didn't even flinch.

It was an epiphany, reshaping how I saw myself. I wasn't a drinker refraining from alcohol - I was simply a non-drinker, and it wasn't a big deal. In fact, it was easy!

You see, we all have a choice. We can either make things difficult for ourselves by dwelling on the challenges ahead, allowing negativity to consume us, or we can choose to believe that it's easy.

The desire for a drink will likely arise at some point. It's a natural part of the journey, but here's the key - resisting that urge is easier than you think. All you have to do is refrain from lifting that glass to your lips. It sounds simplistic, but in reality, it's a powerful act of self-discipline.

Sure, there may be moments when you feel a pang of longing, when you're tempted to give in to the allure of alcohol. You might even feel like you're missing out on the fun, or that you're being perceived as anti-social. But in those moments, remember this - all you have to do, for now, is say no to alcohol. It's as simple as that.

At first, it sounded almost too good to be true to me, too! How could sobriety, something I had struggled with for so long, suddenly become easy? But as I began to embrace this mindset, I realised that it wasn't about denying the difficulties or pretending that everything was perfect. Instead, it was about shifting my focus towards the positive, towards the possibility of feeling good.

By adopting the 'it's easy' mentality, I found myself approaching each day with renewed optimism and determination. Instead of dwelling on past mistakes or worrying about the future, I focused on the present moment, on the small victories and moments of joy that came with each sober day.

Of course, there were still difficulties along the way. Sobriety is never a smooth journey, and there were times when I was challenged. But even in those moments, the 'it's easy' technique served as a guiding light, a reminder that I was capable of overcoming whatever obstacles came my way.

Deciding 'it's easy' is just like flicking a switch in your mind. It can help you get out of that heavy, bogged-down feeling and convince your mind that it really is that easy. Just to be clear, I'm not saying that giving up the booze is, literally, easy, but instead, describing a mind hack that many people have found to be effective.

Quitting alcohol won't be without its struggles. But mindset is everything when it comes to quitting the booze. What level of suffering would you like for yourself on your sobriety journey? Would you like a nine out of ten, or are you more of a three person?

It's worthy of consideration. Most of us don't realise that we have a choice. In sobriety, as in life, you are guaranteed a certain degree of suffering. But we don't need to act as if this is a travesty. If we do, we suffer the fact that we are suffering.

Many of us experience this kind of 'compound suffering' without examining our thought patterns. If we have the grace to accept some degree of suffering as inevitable and choose to reframe, we will find our sobriety journey a lot easier.

This deceptively simple yet powerful strategy has proven to be a game-changer for not just me, but for countless others facing similar challenges. Whenever obstacles loom on the horizon, the mantra 'it's easy' becomes our steadfast companion, guiding us through the toughest of times.

Imagine yourself at a party, surrounded by friends, the familiar scent of alcohol lingering in the air. The temptation to drink may be strong, but armed with the belief that declining is easy, you stand firm in your resolve.

By preemptively deciding that saying no is effortless, you strip away the power of temptation before it even has a chance to take hold.

Sure, there may be moments when you feel a twinge of temptation or doubt creeping in, but in those moments, the simple act of repeating 'it's easy' serves as an anchor, grounding you in your decision and alleviating any unnecessary suffering.

It's flipping that switch, instantly transforming your mindset from one of struggle to one of ease.

And the beauty of it all is that when you approach challenges with a light-hearted attitude, you open yourself up to possibilities and opportunities that you may have otherwise overlooked. Instead of being weighed down by stress and anxiety, you're able to face each challenge head-on, with a smile on your face and a spring in your step.

So, the next time you find yourself confronted with a difficult decision or tempted to veer off course, remember these two simple words -

'It's easy.'

Embrace them wholeheartedly and watch as they pave the way for a brighter, happier, and more fulfilling journey ahead.

Quitting alcohol is challenging enough without increasing your level of suffering by throwing your own pity party. So, make 'it's easy' your aim, and remember, it's not a statement - it's a technique.

Repeat to yourself, 'it's easy.' Let those words sink in, reminding yourself that your mindset plays a significant role in how you perceive and experience challenges. Instead of approaching sobriety with dread or a sense of deprivation, embrace it with optimism and determination.

As the late Dr. Wayne Dyer wisely said, 'If you change the way you look at things, the things you look at change.'

By shifting your perspective and adopting a positive mindset, you'll find that navigating the ups and downs of sobriety becomes a whole lot easier. So, take it one step at a time, and trust that you have the strength and resilience to overcome any obstacle that comes your way.

9.
I'VE GOT A BURNING DESIRE

Danni : When we made the choice to stop drinking, we didn't just sit around bored. With all that newfound time on our hands, we delved into learning new skills, exploring long-neglected hobbies, and simply getting excited by discovering new concepts and new ways of thinking.

Ash threw himself into his passions, running guitar scales, hitting the gym, and riding waves like a maniac. And in the midst of it all, he felt compelled to capture the tales and insights of the true icons who'd conquered the surfing and music worlds.

Pouring his heart and soul into every word, he penned his book Surf by Day, Jam by Night that echoed his passion for both crafts.

I went down the spiritual path, reading or listening to anything that expanded my internal growth. Meditation and gentle yoga became my daily rituals, bringing calm and insight into my life.

There was never any time to be bored because we were filling our cups, not our wine glasses.

Keeping yourself engaged in activities that resonate with you on a personal level is key. For me, taking long walks is a source of immense joy, but Ash isn't particularly fond of them. Instead, he finds solace in running guitar scales, a practice that I absolutely loathe. The key is to indulge in activities that hold significance to you and bring genuine pleasure.

Find ways to reward yourself with pursuits that align with your interests and aspirations. Whether it's honing a skill you're passionate about or indulging in activities that uplift you and make you feel good. Make sure they add value to your life and contribute to your overall well-being.

Do anything that will break that cycle of thinking about alcohol and instead switch the focus. It's essential here to do something that makes you feel good. You won't feel motivated to do something that's a headache. You want to signal to your brain that if you don't succumb to this craving, you're going to get rewarded by getting to do something you really love and enjoy.

The key lies in shifting your mindset, breaking free

from the cycle of obsession, and embracing cravings without fear. They're an inevitable part of the quitting process and are actually a sign that transformation is underway.

Instead of resisting cravings, allow them to come, welcome them with open arms, and view them as signals of progress.

According to Dr. Gabor Maté, it's crucial to adopt a mindful approach to our cravings by accurately identifying them for what they are. Each time we succumb to a craving, we inadvertently reinforce its hold over us. However, by consciously recognising and labelling it as an 'obsessive thought' rather than a genuine need, we gradually diminish its power.

In most cases, when it comes to craving a drink, the sensation typically ebbs and flows over a span of a few minutes to about twenty minutes. Picture it as a wave gradually taking shape - it begins as a gentle ripple and steadily gains momentum, reaching its peak intensity for only a brief moment before subsiding once more.

Understanding this pattern can be empowering, as it highlights the temporary nature of cravings and reminds us that they are transient experiences rather than permanent states of being. By riding out the wave with patience and resilience, we can navigate through cravings more effectively and emerge on the other side with greater strength and resolve.

Don't react whenever you experience a craving. Instead, let it run its natural course. Doing this allows you to change a deep-seated pattern that no longer serves you. It's like doing a mental push-up, and you get stronger each time.

Imagine you wanted to get into shape, so you went to your local gym. You started working out, but every time you felt discomfort in your muscles, you thought it was a sign you should quit.

Instead, successful gymgoers experience a sense of satisfaction when they feel this. They lift the weight, knowing that the discomfort signals that they're on their way to achieving their goals.

Cravings can tend to freak people out, but they become a bigger deal when we resist them. The key is learning to 'allow' the urges to pass through. Notice where you feel these urges in your body and if there's a story in your head going along with them. Notice what emotions are present for you. You can learn so much about yourself in these moments if you stay open and inquisitive.

Observe the mind rather than believing everything it says and see these cravings as a sign of change and opportunity.

Most people believe that a craving precedes a relapse, whereas we see cravings as an inevitable part of quitting. Whenever you don't succumb to a craving, you create new neural pathways that signal to your brain that things are shifting. Remember, change rarely comes out of a comfort zone.

There are many effective ways to help regulate your sympathetic nervous system and disengage from the adrenaline and stress that come with cravings. The first and most effective method is to connect to your breath. Your breath is the quickest way to self-regulate. Focusing on the breath brings you out of your mind, into your body and back into the present moment.

The second most effective technique is to move your body. This connects you to your sensory systems, making you aware of your body and, again, taking you out of your head and back into the present moment.

Take a moment to tune into your body and surroundings. Pay attention to your posture - are you standing tall or slouching? Notice your breathing - is it shallow or deep? Take a few deep breaths to ground yourself.

Look around and observe your environment. What can you see? Take note of the colours, shapes, and textures around you. Listen closely to the sounds in your surroundings - the hum of traffic, the chirping of birds, or the rustling of leaves.

As you become more aware of your surroundings, allow yourself to relax.

You can gently sway from side to side, feeling the rhythm of your movements calming your mind. Place your hands on your chest and belly, feeling the gentle rise and fall of your breath. You can softly pat or rub your chest and belly, offering yourself a soothing touch akin to comforting a child.

Notice the sensations in your body as you engage in these gentle movements and touches. What does it feel like to connect with yourself in this way? Embrace the sensations and let them anchor you in the present moment, providing a sense of calm and grounding amidst any cravings or discomfort.

Do you feel a sense of deepening connection with your own body? As you take a slow, deliberate breath in through your nose and then exhale gently through your mouth with a soft 'shh,' it's almost as if you're cradling your inner child, offering comfort and reassurance. In this moment, allow yourself to embody both the caregiver and the nurtured, recognising that everyone deserves moments of self-soothing and tenderness.

Another great breathing technique is the double-up breath, which we use a few times a day because it's quick and effective. You'll find it quickly becomes part of your everyday toolkit.

When you're feeling stressed, scattered, or overwhelmed, extending and focusing on your exhale will help chill those feelings and settle both the mind and body.

Our exhale is neurologically tied to the relaxation signals in the brain, which is why we sigh when we're relieved. Double-up breathing is a super simple technique that involves breathing into your diaphragm for the count of four and extending your exhalation for the count of eight. If you can't quite make it to a count of four, try breathing in for three and then out for six.

This breathing technique will help you to relax and ease anxiety. When your exhale is even a few counts longer than your inhale, the vagus nerve (running from the neck down through the diaphragm) tells your brain to turn on your parasympathetic nervous system and turn down your sympathetic nervous system. This means you come out of panic or stress mode and into rest and relaxation mode. It's like taking a natural Valium.

The parasympathetic system controls your rest, relax, and digest response. When the parasympathetic system runs the show, your breathing slows, your heart rate returns to a more relaxed pace, your blood pressure lowers, and your body eases back into a state of calm and healing.

On the other hand, if your sympathetic nervous system is running the show, you are ready to fight the sabre-toothed tiger. Your heart races, your blood pressure rises, and you're on high alert. When you're in this state, you're more likely to act out of reaction rather than well-thought-out actions. In this case, that could be reaching for a drink.

Guiding your body into a parasympathetic state is easier than you might think. It just takes a slight tweak of the breath.

So, extend that exhale whenever you remember. In the car, on the loo, doing the dishes, reading this, during work, before sleep, when you wake up. Do it as often as you can to keep yourself level. Whether you feel like a drink or not, make double-up breathing your practice.

★ ★ ★

Box breathing is another powerful technique. Originally developed for the Navy Seals to promote calmness and concentration. It's remarkably straightforward.

Inhale through your nostrils, counting to four, then hold for four, exhale for four, and hold for four again, envisioning equal sides of a box.

As you inhale, visualise travelling up one side of the box. Next, imagine moving across the top of the box while holding your breath. Then, follow the breath down the right side of the box on the exhale and then the bottom of the box while you hold, repeating this four times. This rhythmic pattern can help regulate your nervous system and induce a sense of tranquillity and balance.

By utilising double-up and box breathing techniques, you can tap into your body's natural ability to self-regulate and find calm amidst the storm of cravings. Remember, each breath is an opportunity to signal to your brain that you're in control and that change is not only possible but inevitable.

★ ★ ★

When you wake up tomorrow morning, you might like to add to your self-soothing techniques by starting your day with a series of gentle stretches, allowing your body to awaken gradually as you move through each motion. As you reach your arms overhead, you release the tension that may have built up overnight, inviting a sense of lightness and vitality into your being.

Throughout the day, whenever you feel the onset of cravings or stress, take a moment to pause and stretch. Perhaps it's a simple stretch of the arms and shoulders, or a gentle twist of the torso to release tension in the spine. With each stretch, you reconnect with your body, grounding yourself in the present moment and allowing the mind to find calm amidst the chaos.

Incorporating stretching into your daily routine not only helps to alleviate physical tension but also provides a moment of mindfulness and self-care. It's a gentle reminder to listen to your body's needs and honour them with compassion and kindness.

So, whether you're standing in line at the grocery store or sitting at your desk during a busy workday, take a few moments to stretch. Feel the subtle shifts in your body and the soothing release of tension, knowing that you're nurturing yourself from the inside out. And as you engage in this self-care, remember to also speak nurturing words of support and understanding to yourself.

Take a moment to reflect on the comforting words you may have longed to hear as a child from a trusted adult during times of distress. Whether it's words of reassurance, encouragement, or validation, speak them out loud if possible, allowing your subconscious to absorb their comforting message.

While it may feel unfamiliar or even awkward initially, with practice, this technique becomes increasingly natural and effective.

Remind yourself that you are okay, that you are safe, and that you are deserving of love and care.

Embracing self-nurturing practices like this fosters a deep sense of compassion and tenderness towards yourself.

Even if you've cultivated a tough, rugged exterior, complete with tattoos and a rock 'n' roll attitude, embracing moments of self-nurture isn't a sign of weakness. It's a testament to your inner strength and resilience. By allowing yourself to be soothed in these moments, you're tapping into a profound well of self-awareness and emotional regulation, essential to navigating life's challenges.

As you practise these methods over time, you'll gain a deeper insight into your own needs and assemble a toolkit of strategies to bolster your well-being and kick the cravings for good!

10.
POISON IN THE PUNCH

Ever wondered what really goes on inside your body when you crack open a cold one? Well, get ready to deep dive because we've dedicated this chapter to unlocking the science behind it all.

From the very moment alcohol enters your system, it's like flipping a switch that sets off a chain reaction, touching every corner of your physiology.

We're talking about your brain, liver, and heart - no part of your body is spared from the effects of alcohol.

We won't sugarcoat it - this stuff can be downright terrifying. But trust us, understanding these physiological effects isn't just eye-opening. It's empowering. Armed with knowledge, you can make informed choices about your drinking habits and take proactive steps to protect your health.

And as we uncover the truth about alcohol, you'll gain a newfound respect for the resilience of the human body. Sure, the realities of alcohol's impact can be daunting, but they also highlight the incredible capacity of your body to heal and bounce back.

So, let's get into it! Sit down, strap in and without further ado, let us introduce you to...

Alcohol, also known as ethanol, is a volatile and flammable toxin. It's commonly used for antiseptic, disinfectant, various solvents, and medicines. The most extensive use of ethanol is as a fuel or a fuel additive. When we consider alcohol like this, the fact we drink this stuff for fun is insane!

But how exactly does it affect different parts of our bodies? Let's break it down, as understanding this is the key to sparking change.

The Mouth: Your first sip. 'Now I can finally relax,' says your conditioned brain.

You know a buzz is coming. The alcohol hits your mouth, swishing around, and immediately starts affecting the mucosal tissue. This mucosal tissue lines your oral cavity and tongue, keeping things lubricated and smooth. It's particularly important to speakers and singers to keep the voice box lubricated.

Another of its amazing properties is that it's capable of absorbing alcohol. From your very first sip, the poisonous ethanol has a point of entry straight into your bloodstream, and this is before you've even swallowed.

The Stomach: Down your throat (pharynx), the alcohol goes, past the epiglottis, which blocks off the entry to the windpipe (trachea), cleverly diverting the liquid onto the oesophagus, the pipe that sends the food and drinks into the stomach.

This is the next stop where alcohol gets absorbed into your bloodstream via the mucosal lining of the stomach. Substantially more alcohol is absorbed into your bloodstream here than in the mouth, but far from all of it, and off some more alcohol/ethanol goes, heading straight to the liver.

If you have eaten some food, the stomach's processes will be slower. The pyloric sphincter at the base of your stomach 'bag' will be closed to allow some extra time for the food to break down. If you haven't eaten food, this sphincter is more open, and the alcohol will move quickly through your stomach and into the small intestine.

The Small Intestine: The small intestine is where the vast majority of alcohol absorption will occur, albeit in a slower process.

The mesentery, the incredible lace-like structure that attaches the intestine to your body, is lined with small veins whose primary function is to absorb the nutrients as your food travels through the eighteen-foot (on average) journey through the small intestines.

The small veins of the mesentery absorb the alcohol, sending it into the body's bloodstream, albeit with a more gradual process.

The Liver: The second largest organ in the human body. It serves a range of important and distinct functions and has an amazing capacity to regenerate itself, which sets it apart from other organs.

This regeneration ability is necessary due to the amount of stress the liver undergoes. It acts as the main organ responsible for detoxifying the body and removing toxins from the system.

Apart from ethanol, there are other toxic nasties that get into your digestive tract and end up in your liver to be converted and de-toxified. Junk food, preservatives, additives, plastics, and heavy metals being just a few.

Your heroic liver detoxifies what is dumped on it with some complicated and magical chemistry.

Once the alcohol/ethanol gets to the liver, it meets up with an enzyme called alcohol dehydrogenase (this enzyme is also produced in the stomach in smaller quantities).

This is the first bit of alchemy when the alcohol dehydrogenase meets the alcohol/ethanol and converts it into the carcinogen, acetaldehyde.

The liver will not be outsmarted by this poisonous acetaldehyde, and it quickly converts it to acetate, which is okay for the body. The problem lies with the amount of ethanol consumed vs time spent consuming it.

After only one drink an hour, your liver is backing up with unconverted acetaldehyde. It then overloads, sending the unconverted ethanol-laden blood to the heart, which sends it on to the lungs.

The Lungs: The ethanol-laden blood goes into the lung tissues via the delicate lacework of the bronchial tree's blood supply.

The ethanol permeates the organ and evaporates into the air sacks in your lungs, to be eliminated via your breath. This is what creates your booze breath.

No toothbrush can wash it away. When you blow into a breathalyser at a roadside breath test for alcohol, this is what is being measured. You are actually breathing out ethanol. It's just one small way your body is expelling the poison.

However, there's too much ethanol to be expelled merely through your respiratory system. So, back this toxic blood goes to your heart, which, as it contracts, sends more ethanol-laden blood into your brain, and from there, it's distributed to the whole body.

Keep in mind that wherever the ethanol goes in your body, it's affecting the proteins, de-naturing and dissolving them and compromising membrane tissue. As ethanol gets into your muscles, it affects protein synthesis.

That's one for the bodybuilders and yoga fans to remember, ethanol prevents proteins from being built in the muscle tissue, so if you go to the gym or do a workout and then follow it up with a few drinks, you will be impacting your muscle gains.

The Brain: Ethanol affects the neurological tissue in the brain, specifically the neurotransmitters. These neurotransmitters are responsible for communication between different systems in the brain, and there are billions of connections that occur via them.

Ethanol affects the feel-good neurotransmitters, dopamine and serotonin, which increase pleasure. It also increases the secretion of endorphins. However, ethanol also has negative effects, such as lowering inhibitions, cognition, and reflexes.

This is the feel-good-party-time for the drinker. It's also when judgement starts to be distorted, the prefrontal cortex has checked out, and you're on fire. You may get mouthy, jump on the table to sing too loudly, start an argument with a friend's neighbour or flash your tits at the work Christmas party...you know the drill. Fill in the blanks.

By this stage, your ability to make good choices is impaired. But the ethanol-laden blood is still moving through your body and has far from completed its journey!

As it moves through the brain, your hormonal system is about to be poisoned.

The hypothalamus and the pituitary gland work together, forming the hypothalamic-pituitary axis. These two structures, working in magical harmony together in the brain, control the hormonal system of your entire body.

The hypothalamus is regulating the pituitary gland. This remarkable part of your brain is constantly monitoring your body. If you are drinking, the hypothalamus knows it, and starts adjusting its messages to the pituitary gland. It starts to secrete hormones that inform the pituitary gland to activate your adrenal glands, which secrete the stress hormones cortisol and adrenaline.

The sympathetic nervous system gets aroused, and adrenaline is distributed throughout the body. This leads to an increase in heart rate, which in turn pushes the ethanol-laden blood faster through the vascular system.

Your systems are working hard now, and things have started speeding up. You're starting to sweat more as your body begins to sit in a fight-or-flight mode. It's funny that we think drinking relaxes us when, scientifically, it's doing the opposite, but by the time it's happening, you are so disconnected from your body's subtle language.

Meanwhile, the pituitary gland is simultaneously further affected by the ethanol and slows down the secretion of the anti-diuretic hormone (ADH). This hormone usually maintains the balance of fluids in your body by preventing excessive urination. However, when the ADH secretion slows down, you tend to urinate more than usual and lose water and sodium from your system.

The ethanol in the alcohol has a major impact on the pituitary gland and causes dehydration. This problem is then passed on to the kidneys.

The Kidneys: The kidneys are two bean-shaped organs that are reddish-brown in colour and measure about twelve centimetres on average. They contain thousands of tiny filters that remove toxins from the blood.

Despite their complexity, the kidneys can be described as organs that filter blood into urine. The blood enters through the renal artery, and the waste is then sent to the bladder. In simple terms, urine is blood that has passed through the kidneys.

The kidneys are responsible for filtering toxins, regulating the volume of various fluids and electrolytes, and maintaining acid balances in the body, among other essential functions.

The first problem ethanol is causing here is the reduction of the anti-diuretic hormone, which leads to the dehydration and constriction of blood vessels inside the kidneys, also known as vasopressin. This results in dryness and constriction of the body's systems.

When your blood vessels constrict, less blood is filtered into urine, resulting in fewer toxins being expelled. The low level of anti-diuretic hormone in your system means that ethanol is removing liquid at a faster rate than you are consuming it.

When you consume alcohol, you may notice that you need to urinate frequently. This is because water is being eliminated from your cells and from your entire system. You may have heard the phrase 'breaking the seal' - once you go for your first pee, you usually need to keep running to the bathroom all night.

On top of that, the kidneys are underperforming and overwhelmed and begin to drop electrolytes into the urinary tract. Electrolytes attract water to stay in your body. You literally urinate out the electrolytes, hindering your ability to rehydrate.

If you think you can save yourself by drinking those three big glasses of water before you crash out, well, sorry to disappoint you. It won't work because you already peed out your electrolytes during the last twenty trips to the loo.

And here comes the hangover. After what we know so far, the hangover starts to make sense, right?

The Hangover: Surprisingly, the 'science' is a bit vague at this point. Most suspect that the leading culprit of that dreadful hangover feeling is the acetaldehyde that has accumulated in your system, helping to exacerbate the symptoms of headaches, diarrhoea, nausea, fatigue, or worse that you may be dealing with. It's obvious that it's also because you are dehydrated and your body is a bit beaten up, perhaps after falling off that table.

There are various hangover cures people try and swear by. Salty, greasy food, a raw egg, Gatorade, coffee, a shower, and sleep.

All that is actually scientifically proven is that the cure for a hangover is waiting it out, waiting for your poor body to eliminate the last of the ethanol and acetaldehyde.

What we call a hangover is actually your body responding to a myriad of reactions to the toxic ethanol you have ingested, creating carcinogens in the process.

As the years roll by, if you drink to excess every weekend, these effects accumulate. By the time you get to your thirties and forties, you can really feel it. You don't bounce back quite as quickly, and the hangovers get longer and harder to shake off.

We vaguely blame ageing for this, but not so often do we blame the accumulative effects of regular ethanol ingestion.

Is this an indication of how expertly our culture and advertising have trained us not to see the culprit right before our very eyes? Are they gaslighting us?

Understanding how alcohol travels through your body is like turning on a light switch. It may surprise you, but it's a wake-up call you can't ignore. From the moment you take a sip, alcohol starts affecting your body in various ways.

Bone tissue is safe, but everything else in your body, every organ and muscle, your gallbladder, spleen, kidneys, liver, veins, and blood, can be affected and effectively poisoned by ethanol.

This is why there is no standard for how it affects people. Anyone with existing impairments in any body part will be affected by the ethanol differently. Generally, women are affected quicker than men, but it's not always the case. Age, genetics, lean body mass, overall health, and what you've just eaten will all impact how well your body can convert and expel the poison.

Whether it's disrupting your proteins or affecting your ability to think, its impact is all-encompassing.

So, next time you go to crack open a cold one, think twice about the shitstorm it's about to cause inside of you.

11.
HANGXIETY

Now that you've got a bit of insight into how alcohol plays havoc with your body's inner workings, let's zoom out and take a wider look.

We're not just talking about how it affects you personally but how it ripples out into society at large. From the health implications to the way it messes with our mental well-being, alcohol's impact is far-reaching and often underestimated.

So, let's dig into the numbers, peel back the layers, and see just how much this stuff shapes our world. It's not just about health - it's about our communities, our relationships, and our very way of life.

Ready to dive in?

Did you know that alcohol consumption is responsible for three million deaths every year worldwide, according to The World Health Organisation? This represents 5.3% of all deaths.

Shockingly, for people aged twenty to thirty-nine, alcohol accounts for 13.5% of all deaths.

Just re-read that last sentence to let that sink in.

Men make up 7.7% of global alcohol-related deaths, while women account for 2.6%.

Collectively, smoking, alcohol and illicit drug use kills 11.8 million people globally each year. To put that into perspective, that is more than the number of deaths annually from all the cancers put together.

A lot of these alcohol-related deaths are sadly preventable and are due to road accidents, violence, and suicide.

We're told so often that cigarettes are harmful to our health and cancer-causing. Still, somehow, alcohol has been able to dodge that particular label despite also being responsible for lung cancers, colorectal cancers, cancers of the mouth and throat, oesophageal cancers, and pancreatic, breast and liver cancer.

In a recent Lancet Oncology study, heavy or risky drinking was defined as two drinks or more per day. This doesn't seem like much. However, just this amount of drinking accounted for 85% of new alcohol-related cancers.

Back in the day, we used to shrug off alcohol as something that might make us a bit fat or maybe be a bit harsh on our liver. We didn't give much thought to those regular two to three drink nights we had about four to five times a week. They were the ones we saw as almost inconsequential, just a couple of drinks to unwind.

But now, armed with more knowledge, it's like seeing things in a new light. We're starting to grasp the true impact those seemingly harmless nights had on us. It's quite an eye-opener, isn't it?

We didn't decide to quit solely for the sake of our health - I mean, let's face it, our diet wasn't exactly spotless either. The truth is, we made the decision because our binge drinking was getting out of hand. But when we look at the stark statistics, it's like a wake-up call, reminding us how fortunate we were to have made that choice.

One old rocker, who has dearly departed, told us, 'No one gets away with it,' nodding towards his trusty pack of rollies. He was eventually diagnosed with oral cancer and sadly died a year later. Everyone blamed the ciggies for it, and the fact that he'd had at least four to five beers every night for the past thirty years didn't even get a mention.

Regular drinking, every night or even a big session on the weekend, can create a dependency cycle, where you train your brain to feel rewarded by the alcohol, depending on it to give you a dump of dopamine. It feels good, especially considering you've been experiencing a dopamine deficit due to your last big session. This is the all too familiar cycle.

This dopamine deficit often leads to feelings of overwhelming anxiety. Beyond Blue states, according to studies, that on average, one in four people will suffer from anxiety, approximately one in five men and one in three women.

Anxiety is not just a case of everyday worrying. It's natural to have some amount of worry in our daily lives. Anxiety is when this worried state spills over into everyday life and cannot be shut off.

Alcohol is not the only cause of anxiety. However, it does fuel it, so if you're currently feeling anxious, the last thing your body needs is more alcohol. Drinking is like putting petrol on the fire of anxiety.

★ ★ ★

Danni : Ever since I was a teenager, I've suffered from huge panic attacks. They would come out of nowhere and literally cripple me, and I often thought I was going mad or was going to die. There were times when I'd be having a panic attack or feel one coming on, so I'd drink to make it stop.

They got a little better as I got older. However, it

wouldn't be uncommon for me to wake Ash up in the middle of the night when I was pacing the floor with a racing heart, asking him to talk to me until it passed.

When I stopped drinking, the panic attacks disappeared. Like, I literally haven't had one since. I don't know if it was the work I did on my mindset, getting more quality sleep, or removing alcohol...maybe it was the combo? But I do know they stopped.

One of the main tools I recommend for people suffering from anxiety is to cultivate a mindfulness and meditation practice. Research has shown that simply being mindful can boost your immune system, reduce cognitive decline, help your heart health, improve sleep and reduce anxiety.

Although we all have different reasons for drinking, there is a common theme among those who like getting drunk - we escape our minds.

Drinking never solves the problems in our daily lives. In fact, it compounds them, but for that brief moment, we have a reprieve from our incessant thinking. Drinking alcohol interrupts the stream of constant thinking that drives us batshit crazy.

Looking back, we can see that, in a sense, drinking served its purpose in giving us that break, which would be fine if it didn't carry with it the ability to ruin our lives.

So, what's the game plan if you're looking to kick the drinking habit? Do you just let your 'monkey mind' run wild, as the Buddhists might say? Well, not quite. It's more about finding ways to tame that inner chimp and steer it towards calmer waters.

Our minds constantly run the show, connecting thought after thought with no full stops. So many of us live in a constant state of reactivity, being pushed and pulled by the thoughts and emotions we experience.

We are controlled by a voice in our head that worries about everything that can go wrong, criticises us for everything we do wrong, and feels guilty or angry about everything that went wrong. This voice interprets every situation instantaneously, and we don't question it.

The good news is we can learn to gain control of the voice by developing awareness. The process of becoming aware is through the practice of mindfulness. I often talk about becoming the observer of your thoughts, and that's exactly what you need to do.

When you become a conscious observer of your thoughts, it's like waking from a dream. When you're aware, you can challenge your thoughts. You start to realise that just because you're thinking them, doesn't mean they're true.

This is particularly helpful when you're giving up alcohol because a massive part of giving up the booze is being able to control your emotions and behaviours without the crutch of alcohol.

Part of being mindful is also about accepting how you feel, not judging your feelings but observing them without labelling them. It's about simply acknowledging those thoughts and feelings without trying to change them.

What messages can you gain from them?

Our bodies hold a wealth of wisdom, and by tuning into our emotions and paying attention to them, we can uncover valuable insights into ourselves, and the motivations behind our actions, rather than merely reacting impulsively.

The secret to developing a daily mindfulness practice is consistency. Here are some simple yet powerful practices you can try out every day. Even if you only spend three minutes on these practices each day, you'll start to see some big changes over time.

Take a moment to become fully present and attentive. Start by focusing on your breath, noticing its rhythm and flow.

Can you slow it down?

Feel the air moving in and out of your nostrils and try to extend your exhales. After a few breaths, check in with yourself.

How are you feeling in this moment?

Take stock of any physical sensations you're experiencing. If you encounter any discomfort, simply acknowledge it without judgment and remind yourself,

'I am safe. I am loved.'

Become aware of your breath again. Try to slow it down and take a few long, conscious breaths. Take one or two double-up breaths, breathing in for a count of four and out for eight. Let everything relax on the out-breath. As you know, long, slow breaths into your diaphragm activate the parasympathetic nervous system, which signals your brain to relax.

Now, take a moment to focus on your senses.

What can you feel, hear, smell, see and taste?

Throughout the day, take a moment to become aware while you're doing a task. So often, we do things on autopilot and let our subconscious run the show. When you're pouring a glass of water, cooking, walking, or driving, be present.

Say in your mind, 'I'm pouring a glass of water,' and focus on the actions required to pour the water.

For example, you might be in the shower and thinking about the heat on your skin, the smell of the soap, the sound of the water, and the taste of toothpaste in your mouth. Take a few deep breaths and smile to yourself, enjoying the moment.

Transform your meals into opportunities for mindfulness by savouring each bite with full awareness. Engage all your senses as you eat, noticing the colours, textures, smells, and flavours of your food. Chew slowly and pay attention to the act of eating, appreciating the nourishment it provides to your body.

Turn your daily walks into opportunities for mindfulness by bringing your attention to the present moment. Feel the ground beneath your feet with each step, notice the sights and sounds around you, and connect with the rhythm of your breath. Walking mindfully can help you feel grounded and centred, even amidst the hustle and bustle of daily life.

A daily meditation practice also improves mindfulness and helps you gain control over your thought patterns. There are loads of meditation techniques, but essentially, you want to take some time out of each day to find a quiet space and focus on your breathing and the sensations in your body.

Take a few moments to scan your body from head to toe, paying attention to any areas of tension or discomfort. Start with your toes and gradually work your way up to the crown of your head, bringing awareness to each part of your body. As you encounter sensations, allow them to be without judgment or the need to change them.

As thoughts and emotions come in, see if you can also observe them without judgment. The idea is to cultivate the ability to simply be with your breath and your body.

Sometimes, the meditation is sitting quietly, but not always. Many people find themselves in a meditative state when appreciating a beautiful piece of art, listening to calming music, or going for a walk in nature.

You might find yourself in this state when surfing a perfectly clear wave, dancing, or admiring a beautiful sunset. These things can act as a doorway to your spirituality and your own sense of the divine. The idea is to be fully present for these experiences and appreciate things that are bigger than Self.

As you continue your journey, may you find moments of stillness amidst the chaos, clarity amidst the confusion, and peace amidst the turmoil. Embrace each moment with an open heart and a curious mind, recognising that every instance of mindfulness presents a chance to root yourself in the present and embrace life to the fullest.

12.
THE POWERS THAT BE

Danni: One particularly horrible morning, I found myself waking up in a daze, feeling like I'd been hit by a freight train. The room was spinning, and my head was throbbing. I tried to piece together the events of the night before, but it was like trying to catch smoke with my bare hands. Everything was a blur, a hazy mess that I couldn't quite grasp.

As I tried to make sense of it all, this overwhelming sense of despair hit me. It was like a wave washing over me, pulling me under with its weight. And to top it off, there was that pounding headache, the trademark of a brutal hangover, reminding me of every bad decision I'd made the previous evening.

It felt like an emotional tsunami crashing down on me, overwhelming and relentless. In that moment, I couldn't ignore the magnitude of what I was experiencing. It was as if I'd finally hit rock bottom, the culmination of countless struggles and battles with alcohol.

I remember feeling so incredibly overwhelmed by this horrible sense of desperation that I just didn't know what to do. I ended up sending a silent plea out into the universe, frantically crying out for help from whoever or whatever might be listening.

I prayed like I'd never prayed before. That's how desperate I was for a way out of the same old cycle that had been dragging me down for way too long.

And you know what? That moment turned out to be life-changing for me. My simple plea to the universe sparked this massive transformation in how I saw things, especially when it came to spirituality.

It's funny how life works sometimes, isn't it? One minute, you're stuck in the same old rut, and the next, you're on this wild journey of self-discovery and growth.

That moment of reaching out and asking for help opened up this whole new world for me, filled with possibilities I never even knew existed.

Exploring avenues for recovery often leads to encounters with concepts like a higher power, universal energy, or Source. While these terms may resonate deeply with some, others may find themselves grappling with scepticism or confusion.

The idea of connecting with a higher power can feel daunting, especially for those who have yet to explore spirituality or who hold reservations about organised religion.

Yet, the essence of tapping into a higher power goes beyond religious dogma or traditional beliefs. It's about accessing a source of strength and guidance that exists beyond our individual selves. This force supports us on our journey towards healing and transformation.

Each person's journey to sobriety is unique, and the sources of spiritual connection and guidance vary widely. Some may find solace in religious practices or rituals, while others may discover spiritual meaning through mindfulness, meditation, or other contemplative practices.

Ultimately, the path to sobriety often involves cultivating a deeper understanding of oneself and one's place in the world, whether that comes from connecting with nature, tapping into a sense of collective consciousness, or finding guidance from within.

Navigating this aspect of recovery requires an open mind and a willingness to explore new perspectives. It's an invitation to delve into the depths of our beliefs and experiences, to uncover the threads that connect us to something greater than ourselves.

While the path may feel scary and uncertain, it also offers the promise of profound insight and spiritual growth.

Whether you're on this journey alone, starting a 12-step program, or seeking guidance from a sober coach or counsellor, embracing the concept of a higher power can be a transformative step on the journey to sobriety. It's an opportunity to cultivate a sense of trust in the unseen forces that guide our lives and discover the reservoirs of strength and resilience within each of us.

★ ★ ★

When I first started exploring the idea of getting sober and reading about spirituality, all the talk about God kind of freaked me out.

I grew up in a family that dragged me to Pentecostal meetings every Sunday. Those gatherings could be quite intense, especially for a child. There was lots of shouting, praying, and people getting all worked up. But instead of feeling inspired, I just felt weirded out.

Those Pentecostal services left a mark on me, and not necessarily a good one. The whole vibe was overwhelming, and I couldn't shake off the uncomfortable feeling it left me with. So, when I started hearing about finding a higher power as part of getting sober, I was hesitant. The last thing I wanted was to dive back into that world of intense religious fervour.

But as I kept figuring out what spirituality meant to me, I realised that my aversion to God talk wasn't about rejecting spirituality altogether. It was more about untangling the mess of my past experiences and fears that had built up over the years.

As I delved deeper, I started to view spirituality as this deeply personal and individual experience. It wasn't about following a set of rules or adhering to a specific religious tradition anymore. Instead, it became about tapping into my own inner wisdom and connecting with something greater than myself in a way that felt authentic and meaningful.

Sure, my path might look different from what I grew up with, but that's okay. I've learned to embrace spirituality in my own way, on my own terms. While it's been a journey full of ups and downs, it's also been incredibly freeing to let go of old baggage and discover a deeper sense of connection with myself and the world around me.

So, does sobriety mean you need to hit the church pew

or get on your hands and knees in front of a crucifix?

Absolutely not! Sobriety doesn't come with a requirement to start attending church services or bowing down in front of religious symbols. The beauty of the sober journey is that it's deeply personal and unique to each individual. So, if spirituality is part of your path to sobriety, it's all about finding what resonates with you.

For some people, that might mean finding solace in nature, connecting with the universe, or simply embracing a sense of gratitude for the present moment.

Others might find comfort in exploring meditative movement practices such as Tai Chi, Qigong, or walking meditation. These practices combine gentle physical movement with mindfulness and breath awareness, promoting relaxation, balance, and inner peace.

The key is to explore different avenues and discover what feels right for you. It's about tapping into something greater than yourself, whether you call it Source, the universe, or simply your own inner wisdom.

By doing so, you can unearth a deeper sense of purpose and reconnect with your true self along the way. So, while sobriety doesn't require a one-size-fits-all approach to spirituality, opening yourself up to the possibility of something beyond the physical realm can be a powerful tool on your journey to healing and self-discovery.

But how exactly do we tap in?

Well, think of recovery as a journey of rediscovery - a quest to reclaim what was once lost. And what's often lost in the turmoil of addiction is our sense of self.

We may have veered so far off course that we've lost sight of who we truly are, buried beneath layers of substance abuse and its accompanying struggles. But through the process of recovery, we embark on a mission to uncover and reclaim our authentic selves, peeling away those layers to reveal the essence of who we are at our core.

Your spiritual journey may encompass various practices, such as a daily gratitude ritual where you reflect on the blessings in your life, acknowledging the abundance that surrounds you.

Additionally, mindfulness exercises allow you to cultivate awareness of the present moment, fostering a deeper connection with yourself and the world around you.

Through acts of compassion, you can extend

kindness and empathy to others by looking for opportunities to offer support, encouragement, and assistance to those in need. This could be through volunteering at a local charity, helping a friend or stranger, or simply offering a kind word or gesture.

Cultivate a spirit of generosity and empathy, recognising the interconnectedness of all beings and the profound impact of small acts of kindness on the world around you.

Seek out opportunities to connect with like-minded individuals who share your spiritual values and aspirations. You might like to join a spiritual or religious community, attend group meditation sessions or workshops, or participate in online forums and discussion groups. Surround yourself with supportive and inspiring individuals who uplift and empower you on your spiritual journey, fostering a sense of belonging, connection, and mutual growth.

Create a vision board to visually represent your goals, dreams, and aspirations. Gather images, words, and symbols that resonate with your desires and arrange them on a board or canvas. Place your vision board in a prominent place where you can see it daily, allowing it to inspire and motivate you to manifest your intentions.

Expressing yourself creatively like this can be a form of meditation and self-discovery, allowing you to tap into your intuition and inner wisdom. Engage in creative activities that bring you joy, such as painting, writing, dancing, or whatever frees your inner artist.

Listen to soulful and uplifting music while you do it, something that nourishes your spirit and uplifts your mood. Whether it's classical music, devotional chants, or soothing melodies, allow yourself to be transported by the healing power of music.

On the flip side, also dedicate time to silent retreats or self-imposed periods of silence. Silence allows you to quiet the noise of the external world and listen to the wisdom of your inner voice. Sit in silence each day for a short amount of time, drop into your heart space, focus on your breath, and imagine yourself letting go of your mind and physical body.

When you find yourself in that mindful moment, take a deep breath and set a simple yet powerful intention for the day ahead. Make a conscious decision to navigate the day with an open heart, filled with compassion and kindness not only for yourself but also for every individual you encounter along the way.

Let this intention guide your thoughts, words, and actions, infusing each moment with warmth and understanding. Embrace the opportunity to spread positivity and goodwill, knowing that even the smallest gestures can make a significant difference in someone else's day.

Trust your inner voice to lead you towards the practices and beliefs that most authentically align with your values and aspirations.

It's okay to try new things.

It's okay to stumble.

It's okay to learn along the way.

While it may seem a little daunting or unnatural at first, we promise it will become easier and easier. You'll begin to really cherish and look forward to those moments of connection, and they'll become the highlight of your day.

Your path to sobriety is uniquely yours, and as you gain confidence in your journey, you'll find yourself becoming more grounded in your own truth. This is a significant milestone, as it signifies a deepening sense of self-awareness and authenticity.

Remember, sobriety is not just about abstaining

from alcohol - it's also about rediscovering who you are at your very essence without the substance acting as your mask.

Trust in your own wisdom and intuition, and you'll find that you already possess everything you need.

13.
LEAVING THE CULT

> 'IF YOU FOLLOW THE HERD,
> YOU'LL END UP STEPPING IN SHIT.'
> **DR. WAYNE W. DYER**

A few months into our sobriety, a funny thing began to happen. Friends, well-meaning as they were, started to raise their eyebrows and drop not-so-subtle hints about our newfound lifestyle. 'You're not going to last,' they'd say with a smirk, or 'Come on, just one won't hurt.' It was as if our decision to abstain from alcohol was seen as some sort of personal affront to their own habits.

At first, these comments hit us like a sucker punch, planting seeds of doubt in our minds and causing us to question our resolve. We grappled with feelings of inadequacy and wondered if maybe we were missing out on something after all. But as time passed and our commitment to sobriety solidified, we came to realise something profound - their doubts were not our burden to bear.

For those facing similar hurdles on the road to sobriety, here are our two cents - stick to your guns and don't let anyone rain on your parade. Your journey to sober living is your own, and nobody else's opinion matters as much as your own determination.

Trust in your inner strength, believe in your ability to bounce back, and know that you've got what it takes to handle whatever comes your way. Just keep putting one foot in front of the other, and remember, you're the captain of your ship, steering it towards calmer waters with every sober step.

Just keep reminding yourself that what you're doing is for your own benefit, not to please anyone else. Your sobriety is a personal journey, and the only person you need to answer to is yourself. All you have to do is stay away from alcohol. Other people's opinions about your choices are irrelevant because they're not the ones walking in your shoes.

As time goes by and you put more distance between yourself and your last drink, you'll start to see things more clearly. You'll realise that a lot of your drinking, especially those wild binge sessions, was just about going along with the crowd, trying to fit in, and chasing a fleeting sense of belonging. But now, you're forging your own path, and that's something to be proud of.

Many people fall off the well-intentioned wagon of sobriety due to people pleasing.

It's a common story - the well-meaning resolve to stay sober at an event like a wedding or a party, only to find yourself caving under the pressure to please others.

You might have gone into it with the best of intentions, swearing off alcohol for the night, but then someone offers you a drink, and you hesitate. You worry about what they'll think if you decline.

Will they judge you for not joining in?

Will they think you're being boring or antisocial?

Or maybe you're just dreading the awkward conversation that might follow if you have to explain why you're not drinking.

The fear of being seen as judgmental or not fun can be overwhelming, and it's easy to give in to the pressure to fit in. But it's important to remember that your sobriety is more important than anyone else's opinion of you. It's okay to say no to alcohol, even if it means facing a few uncomfortable moments. In the end, staying true to yourself is always worth it.

Danni: Quitting alcohol gave me many gifts, but the best gift of all was that I was able to see my people-pleasing tendencies. At first, not being able to hide behind alcohol highlighted a lack of confidence I didn't even know I had.

It showed up in every social interaction, and I had no choice but to deal with it. I'd say out loud, 'I'm feeling a bit uncomfortable right now, and that's okay.'

You might have heard of the 'name it to tame it' idea. Well, it works! When you can put a name to what you're feeling, suddenly it doesn't seem so overwhelming.

So, picture this - you're at a party, feeling a bit out of place and vulnerable. It's uncomfortable, sure, but it's not the end of the world. You ride out those first ten minutes of cravings, and before you know it, they start to fade away. You settle into the moment, and hey, sometimes you even end up having a blast. It's all about pushing through that initial discomfort and giving yourself the chance to enjoy the experience.

Over time, my confidence started to grow. That's a real feeling of freedom, and the more I felt that freedom, the more I wanted to hang on to it. I gave less fucks what people thought about the fact that I wasn't drinking and realised that what they thought was more a measure of where they were at, not where I was at.

Embarking on the journey of sobriety can often feel like navigating uncharted territory, especially when your social circles revolve around alcohol-fuelled gatherings and late-night escapades. It's natural to feel a sense of isolation at first, like you're the odd one out in a sea of continuous partying. But as you commit to your newfound path, something remarkable begins to happen.

Your true friends, the ones who truly care about your well-being, they start to show themselves.

They may stumble a bit at first, unsure of how to relate to this new version of you. But in time, they come to accept and even embrace the changes you're making. And as your relationships evolve, so too do your social activities.

Gone are the days of wild nights out and boozy brunches. Instead, you find yourself enjoying quieter, more meaningful moments with your friends.

Spending your weekends going for long walks in the park or hosting cosy gatherings at your place, complete with cups of steaming hot tea and heartfelt conversations. And while it may take some getting used to, this new way of connecting feels authentic, fulfilling, and, most importantly, sustainable.

I actually went back to Castlemaine recently and caught up with my old core group of drinking buddies. I had some alcohol-free bubbles, and they all had alcoholic drinks. I initially felt uncomfortable being the odd one out, but that quickly passed.

We made homemade pizzas, listened to music, danced, talked and had a great night. All the elements were there with the people I love, but I wasn't drinking alcohol. I had a great time, and alcohol got no credit for my good time.

★ ★ ★

At what stage in our life did we start to believe we could only have fun when alcohol was involved? A child doesn't need alcohol to have fun, and kids know how to have fun more than anyone.

So, when did we start to limit ourselves?

When did we start believing we could only have a good time if it included alcohol?

In truth, alcohol has had one of the best marketing teams known to humankind. It's been sold to us as the ultimate enhancer of life's experiences since we were barely out of nappies. From flashy commercials to glamorous product placements in movies and TV shows, the message has been hammered into our heads - alcohol equals good times.

We're led to believe that we need it to celebrate birthdays, toast to achievements, or simply unwind after a long day. But that is such bullshit!

The joy, the laughter, and the connection we attribute to alcohol? It's not the booze doing the heavy lifting - it's us. We've been conditioned to believe that alcohol enhances our experiences, but in reality, it often detracts from them.

When we're not drinking, we're more present. We're truly engaged when people share their stories, we savour every bite of our food, and we're tuned in to the music and atmosphere around us. It's like life suddenly becomes more vivid and vibrant.

Plus, we're sharper and quicker with our wit, and those one-liners just seem to roll off the tongue effortlessly. Sober living isn't about missing out - it's about experiencing life in high definition!

This new level of presence was one of the biggest reasons I never wanted to return to where I was before. I had this vision for myself and the person I wanted to become. I would see myself as confident, happy and empowered. I would see myself at dinner parties chatting away happily while drinking soda water and imagine how I'd feel the next day waking up, having not made a fool out of myself.

Seeing myself as the person I wanted to become became part of my daily practice.

In his book *Breaking the Habit of Being Yourself*, Joe Dispenza mentions that we can create change in our brains just by mentally rehearsing what we want to experience. Research shows that people who mentally rehearse what they want to happen before the event occurs have a far greater success rate when the actual event occurs.

So, when you're heading off to your cousin's wedding, and you're worried about being triggered to drink, start imagining yourself already there. Imagine you're saying no to that drink and see yourself happily walking to the dance floor with all the confidence in the world. Or contentedly chatting with Aunty Marge over a delicious mocktail, knowing that you'll be waking up fresh as a daisy, not having to worry about your actions from the night before.

Dr. Wayne Dyer's wisdom rings true.

'As you think, so shall you be.'

It's a powerful reminder that our thoughts shape our reality. So, why not take the reins and start steering your thoughts in the direction of the person you want to become?

But here's the thing - don't stop at just thinking about it. Immerse yourself in the feeling of embodying that ideal version of yourself. Close your eyes and picture it vividly - the confidence, the clarity, the sense of purpose coursing through your veins. Imagine yourself standing tall, empowered, and fully in control of your destiny.

As you let yourself sink into that vision, notice how it makes you feel. Maybe you'll feel a surge of excitement, a tingling sensation of anticipation, or perhaps even a sense of calm knowing that you're finally aligning with your true values.

Embrace those feelings, relish in them, and let them fuel your journey. And don't be afraid to crack a smile as you bask in the glow of your imagined success. After all, every great journey begins with a single thought.

Try and channel this newfound vision of yourself into your behaviours and values. Remember, you tend to feel unhappy and dissatisfied when your behaviour and actions don't match your values. When they do align, you cultivate a sense of direction and well-being as you strive to be the best possible version of yourself.

Think about the person you want to be going forward in sobriety.

How can you live your life more in alignment with your values?

When you must make a choice, ask yourself if it aligns with your values. The more you do this, the more you'll get into the habit of making better decisions that make you feel good.

Take a moment to identify your top ten values and write them down.

Whether it's authenticity, family, freedom, or passion, let these values serve as your compass and consider how alcohol may have compromised them. By acknowledging these discrepancies, you empower yourself to redefine your narrative and craft a new label.

If we cling to outdated labels, we're shackled to the past, unable to break free and embrace transformation. Despite our efforts to align with our values and cultivate healthier habits, clinging to the outdated notion of being 'the life of the party' keeps us tethered to a reality that stifles change.

To truly break free from destructive patterns, we must shed these outdated labels and pave the way for new narratives to emerge.

Asking questions about your old labels can help you gain massive insights.

What does this label really mean?

Am I a party animal?

Am I a people-pleaser?

Where does that come from?

Where is my self-worth sitting in the scheme of things?

By shedding these outdated identities and embracing new labels, we shatter the constraints of our old patterns and open ourselves to a world of possibility.

With each step forward, we hold the power to rewrite our story.

Let's make it fucking magical!

14.
MENTORS & MINDSET

When life throws you a curveball, who do you turn to for guidance?

Are your friends your sounding board, or do you seek wisdom from mentors or experts?

Maybe you find solace in endlessly scrolling Google for the answers?

Wherever you find support, rest assured that there is so much wisdom still out there, just waiting for you to find it.

Instead of waiting for answers to fall into your lap, or sitting around feeling lost, actively seek them out. Whether it's chatting with pals, diving into a good book, or tuning in to a podcast, be proactive about finding the resources that speak to your soul.

During our period of self-discovery, we really threw ourselves into our education. We were like sponges, soaking in everything we could listen to or get our hands on. We dived headfirst into books, podcasts, and audiobooks, absorbing every word like thirsty explorers in a vast desert.

We were on a mission, devouring insights from every teacher and expert we stumbled upon. It was an adventure of the mind, a journey where each page turned, and each podcast played became a new chapter in our quest for understanding.

We were high on knowledge, eager to unlock the secrets of addiction psychology and peel back the layers of our own experiences. It was a time of growth and expansion, where every bit of information we consumed added another piece to the puzzle of our personal development.

Danni: I just couldn't get enough of Dr. Wayne Dyer. I'd wake up and go for a walk most mornings and listen to Wayne's podcast over and over. I would watch his YouTube clips, read every book, do his meditations, and listen to him as I drifted off to sleep at night. Dr. Wayne Dyer changed my life. He was exactly what I needed and the spiritual embodiment of where I wanted to be.

Wayne may not be the right fit for everyone, but that's the beauty of this journey - you have the freedom to find your own teacher, someone whose words resonate deeply with your soul. It's about exploring different perspectives, learning from diverse voices, and ultimately finding the guidance that speaks directly to you.

You can start by reading books, listening to podcasts, watching videos, or attending workshops and seminars led by your chosen thought leaders. Seek out topics that interest you, whether it's personal development, mindfulness, spirituality, or something else entirely.

As you immerse yourself in the wisdom of these guides, allow yourself to absorb their teachings and reflect on how they apply to your own life. Take notes, journal your thoughts and insights, and engage in discussions with others who share your interests.

Dive into and explore the transformative teachings of luminaries like Neville Goddard, Eckhart Tolle, and Michael Beckwith, whose profound insights into compassion and mindfulness can brighten your path. Each offers a unique perspective on spirituality and personal growth.

Embrace the empowering wisdom of Tony Robbins, the vulnerability and courage of Brené Brown, and the profound insights into addiction and healing from Dr. Gabor Maté. And don't forget the writings of Michael Singer, whose words can help you transcend the limitations of the mind and discover inner freedom.

You've got a treasure trove of tools right at your fingertips! There's a huge library of quit lit books out there, packed with wisdom and inspiration to guide you on your journey, and some incredible podcasts where you can tune in to hear real people sharing their journeys of triumph over alcohol.

I launched the How I Quit Alcohol podcast back in 2021, honestly not expecting anyone to listen. But lo and behold, it's been a wild ride! Fast forward to today, and it's had over two million downloads worldwide, which completely exceeded my expectations.

What's even more incredible is the huge impact it's had on people. Every day, I receive messages from listeners who've made the life-changing decision to quit drinking after tuning in. Their stories are a testament to the profound effect of hearing other people's journeys toward sobriety.

It's a reminder that we're all in this together, supporting and uplifting one another along the way. So, if you're on the fence about taking the leap, know that you're not alone, and there's a whole community waiting to cheer you on.

Immerse yourself in it. Dive headfirst into this sea of positivity, where every message is a literal ray of sunshine. These mentors, these guides, they're like sturdy lighthouses in the midst of a storm, ready to be your life raft whenever you need them.

While we were on our journey, we made a conscious decision to cut out the noise - the constant barrage of negativity from the news, the gossip, the toxic conversations. Instead, we tuned in to positivity. We surrounded ourselves with uplifting content, inspiring stories, and words that fuelled our souls.

It wasn't an easy shift at first, but it was worth it! Slowly but surely, we felt the weight of negativity lift from our shoulders. We found ourselves smiling more, laughing more, and feeling lighter in spirit. It was like a breath of fresh air for the soul, and it changed everything.

To really soak up all this wisdom and keep your mind open to new ideas, you've got to nurture a growth mindset. It's not just about changing your thinking - it's about transforming the very foundation of how you live your life.

Embracing a growth mindset is like saying 'bring it on' to challenges and seeing them as chances to level up in life.

Setbacks?

They're just blips on the radar, not roadblocks. And when you believe in the magic of putting in the effort and bouncing back stronger, you're unstoppable.

Adopting a growth mindset isn't just about being open to new ideas and learning from your slip-ups. It's about diving into life like an adventurer, eager to seize every opportunity to evolve and become the best version of yourself.

With this mindset, you're not just along for the ride - you're driving the bus and charting your own course.

Your mindset plays a critical role in how you handle life's challenges, influencing your resilience and perseverance. Individuals with a growth mindset demonstrate greater resilience when challenges arise, as opposed to those with a fixed mindset who are more likely to give up.

A fixed mindset is one that assumes abilities or talents are well...fixed. Those with a fixed mindset may not believe that skills or intelligence can be enhanced. Meanwhile, those with a growth mindset believe that these things can be enhanced with persistence and repetition.

Transitioning to a growth mindset is a journey that

requires consistent effort and practice. If you've been stuck in a fixed mindset, constantly telling yourself,

'I'm not good at this' or 'I don't have what it takes' may be holding you back from breaking free from alcohol addiction.

But the good news is that your mindset isn't fixed. Like a muscle, it can be strengthened and trained over time. So, rather than feeling trapped by negative or limiting beliefs, you have the power to shape your mindset into one of growth.

The fundamentals for changing your mindset are simple. Start by paying close attention to your internal dialogue. How you speak to yourself reflects your mindset more than you might realise.

Do you actually believe you can give up alcohol?

It's one thing to want to change, but do you really believe that change is possible?

When we cling to the familiar mindset of

'I can't really do this, I always mess up, I lack willpower, I'm weak,' we subject ourselves to negative self-talk. But with these internal voices, how can we ever expect to change?

I had to change my thinking pretty quickly in those initial twelve months. It was like flipping a switch in my mind. Initially, I was hesitant, unsure if I could truly commit to sobriety. But as time went on, I realised the power of shifting my mindset from uncertainty to unwavering confidence.

It's incredible how simply saying those words out loud - 'Maybe I can' versus 'Absolutely I can' - can evoke such different feelings within you. It's not just about the words themselves, but the conviction and determination behind them that make all the difference.

Read both of those statements out loud and see how you feel.

★ ★ ★

In psychology, self-efficacy refers to an individual's belief in their ability to take the necessary actions to achieve their goals. If you've attempted to quit before without success, don't dwell on it as a failure. Instead, cultivate compassion and view it as a learning opportunity.

Ask yourself, 'What did I learn from this experience?'

Shift your perspective by replacing limiting beliefs with empowering statements.

Instead of saying, 'I can't do this,' say, 'I had a setback, and setbacks are part of it, but every setback is an opportunity for growth.'

Focus on what went well in your week, identify your strengths, and acknowledge the support network you have around you.

Picture yourself two years from now, living the life you've always dreamed of.

What does that look like?

Maybe you're excelling in your career, surrounded by loving relationships, or diving into passions that light you up. Just by noticing the good things in your life and acknowledging your strengths, you're already starting to change your mindset.

Shifting towards positive self-talk and visualisations might seem like small adjustments, but their impact is profound. When you consciously redirect your thoughts towards recognising your potential and inherent worth, you're essentially rewiring your brain. Instead of dwelling on self-doubt or criticism, you're forging new neural pathways that bolster confidence and self-belief.

Also be mindful of the words you speak to others.

As my mum always said, 'Words have wings.'

Just as you're careful with your internal dialogue, it's essential to consider the impact of your speech on others. Make it a habit to highlight the positives in your life and share your achievements with pride.

Self-deprecating comments might seem harmless or even humorous at times, but they can have a significant impact on your mindset and self-esteem. When you belittle yourself or downplay your abilities, you reinforce negative beliefs about your worth and capabilities.

★ ★ ★

Instead of indulging in self-deprecation, focus on cultivating self-compassion and positive self-talk.

Remember, your subconscious mind absorbs everything you say, whether positive or negative. So, by consciously choosing to speak kindly to yourself and refraining from putting yourself down, you're laying the foundation for a healthier and more resilient mindset.

This stuff works. This isn't just some woo-woo concept - it's backed by solid scientific evidence. Positive psychology research has shown time and again that our thoughts and mindset have a direct impact on our lives. We now know that if the inside doesn't change, the outside doesn't change.

Rewiring the brain is no small feat. For years, we've

been feeding it negative self-talk and self-limiting beliefs, thanks in part to the influence of alcohol. We've convinced ourselves that we're not good enough, that we're weak, or that we're somehow flawed. But here's the truth - You are amazing just the way you are.

It's time to kick those negative thoughts to the curb and start rebuilding your self-esteem and confidence from the ground up. It won't happen overnight, but with patience and persistence, you'll start to see the incredible potential that's been there all along.

Believe in yourself because as we've told you before, you are truly perfect just as you are. You just have to start believing it.

15.
RUN OR RISE

Danni: Taking charge of your life is like stepping into a whole new realm of empowerment. It's like shaking off the fear and uncertainty of childhood and stepping up as a fully-fledged adult who's in the driver's seat of their own life.

Instead of feeling like life's just happening to you, you're the one calling the shots. You're not blaming anyone else for where you're at - you're owning it. That's the game-changer right there.

When you start taking responsibility, it's like you're saying, 'Hey, I'm in control here.' You're not waiting for things to happen - you're making them happen. And yeah, it's not always smooth sailing. You'll hit bumps, for sure. But those bumps? They're part of the ride. They're where you learn and grow.

And the best bit? When you own your life, you start seeing things differently. Suddenly, it's not about playing the victim anymore. It's about being the hero of your own story. You're writing your script, making your choices, and living with the consequences - good or bad. But hey, at least they're your consequences.

When life throws us a challenge, it's tempting to slip into the victim mindset of 'Why is this happening to me?' or 'It's not fair!'

But here's the thing - that mindset, it's like quicksand. The more you struggle, the deeper you sink.

But what if, instead of playing the blame game, you asked yourself,

'What's my role in all this?'

It's not about beating yourself up or wallowing in guilt. It's about taking a good, hard look in the mirror.

It's not always easy. Sometimes, it means admitting that maybe you could've handled things differently. Maybe you made a mistake, or maybe you didn't speak up when you should've.

But here's the kicker - that single question 'What's my part in this?' it's like flipping a switch.

Suddenly, you're not a victim anymore. You're not at the mercy of life's whims. You're in the driver's seat, steering your own ship, which takes guts. It takes honesty. It takes owning up to your flaws and imperfections. Each of us has the capacity to own up to our mistakes and learn lessons from any given situation.

Significant transformations occurred in my life when I began to take ownership of my thoughts and actions, embrace change, and dare to ask uncomfortable questions.

For me, taking responsibility wasn't just a concept - it was a journey.

It wasn't always easy. It meant setting boundaries - not just with others, but with myself too. It meant saying no when I needed to, even if it made me uncomfortable.

Self-care became my lifeline. It was about carving out time for me, whether that meant taking long walks in nature, indulging in a long bath, or simply sitting quietly with a cup of tea. It was about nourishing my body, mind, and soul - every single day.

But taking responsibility also meant being open to new ideas, new therapies. It was about exploring different avenues - from mindfulness to meditation, from yoga to journaling. It was an incredibly liberating experience. It was like I was shedding old layers, revealing a truer, more authentic version of myself.

Accepting what role you play in your own life is such a huge step. I remember talking to my good friend and podcast regular Lyndal Hunt about this when she was working through the AA steps, and it was such a lightbulb moment for me.

It's a great question to ask, 'What role do you play in your own life?' It can feel a bit brutal at first, but if you lean into it, it's actually quite liberating, and the more I practised it, the easier it got. Thank you, Lyndal.

If I find myself dwelling on past events and allowing them to control my present reactions or allowing them to keep me feeling stuck, then I have to take ownership of that. It's my responsibility to acknowledge how I let the past affect me and to take steps to move forward.

Similarly, if someone has wronged me and I failed to communicate my boundaries or needs, leading to feelings of resentment, then I must recognise my role in that situation. It's up to me to address these feelings and work towards resolution.

If my actions have caused harm to others, whether intentionally or unintentionally, it's also essential for me to take responsibility and make amends.

I can't shift the blame onto external circumstances or other people. I must face the consequences of my actions and take proactive steps to repair any damage I've caused. This way, I'm recognising and owning up to my role in various situations, which is crucial for personal growth and fostering healthier relationships with not just myself but also the people around me.

Every twist and turn in life presents an opportunity for growth and learning. When we encounter challenges or difficulties, it's important to pause and ask ourselves - 'What can I learn from this experience?'

Each situation carries valuable lessons that can help us evolve and become better versions of ourselves.

Taking ownership of our lives doesn't mean beating ourselves up over past mistakes or shortcomings. Instead, it involves acknowledging the patterns or defence mechanisms that may have contributed to those situations.

Whether we're just beginning to understand our patterns or have been on a journey of self-discovery for some time, every moment offers an opportunity to take ownership of our circumstances.

As we begin to take responsibility for our lives, we

reclaim control from the circumstances that once left us feeling helpless and victimised. A crucial aspect of this process is to continually keep asking ourselves Lyndal's pivotal question -

'What role did I have to play in this?'

This question serves as a powerful anchor for self-reflection and introspection. It prompts us to examine our actions, choices, and attitudes in the context of the situation at hand.

Did we passively allow events to unfold, or did we actively contribute to their outcome?

Were we completely honest with ourselves and others, or did we withhold the truth?

Did we project blame onto others for our own shortcomings, or did we take ownership of our mistakes?

It's also important to confront the ways in which we may have compromised our own well-being and integrity.

Did we allow others to overstep our boundaries, or did we assertively defend them?

Did we remain silent when our instincts urged us to speak up, or did we heed their guidance?

These questions compel us to confront uncomfortable

truths about ourselves and our behaviour.

When we take ownership and responsibility for and of our lives, we are not only empowering ourselves to take back control, we are simultaneously letting go of what we can't control (the past) and letting our pain guide us through to the tender places and find our own wisdom, our own voice.

Right there is the sweet spot that heals us and changes the way we interact with the world. Just like the legendary Farnsy belts out,

'That's freedom.'

And let's be real, you can't argue with Farnsy. The man's always on point.

It's like finding your groove on the dance floor or hitting that perfect note on a guitar solo - it's pure liberation.

But fear often serves as the primary barrier preventing us from fully embracing this liberation. By delving into our fears, we can uncover profound insights and revelations that illuminate the underlying causes of our reluctance to take responsibility. Exploring the root of our fear through introspection is essential.

Start by taking a deep breath and acknowledging the fear you're feeling. Recognise that it's a natural response to certain situations or thoughts and avoiding or suppressing your fear may only make it stronger in the long run. Instead, give yourself permission to feel it without judgment.

Take some time to reflect on what is triggering your fear.

Is it a specific event, a past trauma, or uncertainty about the future?

Understanding the root cause of your fear can help you address it more effectively. You could also try journaling or talking to a trusted friend or therapist to gain some more clarity.

Once you've identified the source of your fear, consider how you can confront it directly. This might involve gradually exposing yourself to the fear-inducing situation or taking small steps to challenge your beliefs about it. Remember that courage isn't the absence of fear but the willingness to act despite it.

Again, don't hesitate to reach out to others for support and encouragement. Talking about your fears with friends, family, or a therapist can provide valuable perspective and help you feel less alone. Sometimes, simply sharing your feelings can be a powerful first step toward overcoming them.

Be gentle with yourself as you navigate your fears. Remind yourself that it's okay to feel afraid and that your feelings are valid. Treat yourself with kindness and understanding, just as you would a friend facing similar challenges.

Remember that overcoming fear is a process - eventually, you'll find yourself at The Crossroads. It's a moment where you have the power to choose how you respond to the fears that arise and challenge the validity of them by asking a simple question.

Would the worst possible outcome truly be as catastrophic as I imagine?

Often, our fears are exaggerated by our imagination, and reality may not be as dire as we first thought. By questioning the basis of our fears, we can begin to see them in a more rational light.

Then comes the crucial decision - Do you succumb to the instinct to,

Fuck Everything And Run,

allowing fear to dictate your actions and hold you back?

Or do you summon the courage to,

Face Everything And Rise,

confronting your fears head-on and embracing the

opportunity for growth and empowerment?

Choosing to face your fears requires courage and resilience. It means stepping out of your comfort zone and embracing discomfort in pursuit of personal growth. It's about recognising that while fear may be a natural response, it doesn't have to control your decisions or limit your potential any longer.

The decision lies squarely in your hands - Will you retreat, or will you elevate?

16.
FEELING THE FEELS.

Danni: After my dad passed away, it felt like the ground had been ripped out from under me. He was more than just a parent - he was my anchor, my guiding light when everything seemed dark. Without him, I felt adrift, lost in a sea of grief and confusion.

The craving to drink hit me hard. It was like my body was screaming for anything to numb the pain, to drown out the sorrow. But deep down, I knew that alcohol wouldn't bring him back. It wouldn't make the pain go away. It would only dull the edges for a while, leaving me feeling emptier and more lost than ever.

But despite the overwhelming urge to drown my sorrows, I knew I had to keep going. I was exhausted, and I was missing him desperately, but I had to work, look after the kids, and release my podcast.

So, I pushed on, one foot in front of the other, forcing myself to keep moving forward even when every fibre of my being wanted to curl up and disappear.

It was exhausting, both physically and emotionally. There were days when I felt like I was barely holding it together, like I was teetering on the edge of a breakdown. But somehow, I found the strength to keep going, to keep putting one foot in front of the other, even when it felt like the weight of the world was pressing down on my shoulders.

One day, out of nowhere, it just came crashing down hard. Everything in me wanted to go to the bottle shop, and at one point, I swear I could taste the wine in my mouth. It was the deepest yearning I have ever felt, this yearning to escape. I just wanted to stop the sadness and the grief. But I knew that going to the bottle shop wasn't an option, and I just had to sit with it and wait it out.

I asked myself what I needed, and then I got into bed, wrapped myself up in a blanket and cried my little eyes out. I howled, rocked back and forth and screamed into my pillow. When I'd finally started to calm down, I kept telling myself that I felt sad because I missed my beautiful dad, and that was okay. I felt spent afterwards, and looking like a pufferfish, I took a long shower. I kept checking in with myself, and the next day, I still felt fragile, but I WAS okay.

Well, not okay... I was grieving, and I was in pain. That's the thing about grief - it demands to be felt, it's big, it's overwhelming, and it's also so potent. But it can be beautiful as it's an expression of the love that you felt for that person.

I'd made it through this pain without using alcohol to numb me. It was a reminder that facing emotions head-on, even when they're tough, is essential for growth and healing. Using alcohol to numb your pain will only slow your healing.

If you find yourself in a similar situation where you have a painful memory or are feeling triggered by something, avoid labelling that uncomfortable feeling as bad. Observe it without judgement and ask yourself, what would it be like to try and resist the urge to get away from this feeling?

Often, when I'm working with someone and they allow their feelings to be welcomed, felt, and explored, they realise the negative feelings can pass. It's like emotions have energy, and the energy needs to run its cycle. Sure, there might be a peak of discomfort, but then it eases off because it's been acknowledged, let go, and not stored up to create more stress in the body.

When stress does appear in the body, some people

feel it in their chest or clench their jaw, tense their shoulders, or feel funny in their tummy. Take a moment to explore how you're feeling next time you find yourself in a moment of stress.

Shut your eyes, take some deep breaths and notice where the sensation, discomfort or raw emotion is in your body. Don't go into the details of the story. Ignore the monkey chatter and just experience your body. Be a curious explorer and try to suspend judgment of yourself. If you find the feelings in your body too overwhelming, remember it's a gentle practice, and it takes time.

This is a good opportunity to take a moment to reflect on how that process felt by journaling.

Was there resistance?

Was there peace?

Was there acceptance?

Notice what the experience was like for you. If it was too hard or too big, it's a good indicator that you may need some extra help, which is a good thing, not a failure. Even identifying that it's too hard for you is a positive step towards healing.

Alcohol is the Band-Aid that delays our healing. It numbs you to the discomfort that is your teacher.

That's right, the discomfort itself is your teacher. It takes courage to meet your own traumatised self, to get into a relationship with it, and to understand it. We are taught to toe the line, pack our trauma away, and get on with life. This serves us to a degree. However, the body holds on to these traumas, which remain stored until we begin addressing them.

Our traumas and discomforts need to be met with love and compassion. We need to not be at war with these aspects of ourselves but try to understand them to unravel them. Some people don't even realise they are there, being carried in their bodies and impacting their behaviour. Other people know they have trauma and realise they self-medicate or self-soothe. In each case, the way forward is the same.

The most important first step to healing is beginning to have a relationship with your internal world. That's where the wounds are stored, and that's where the healing has to happen. It can take a long time, sometimes many years, to slowly and compassionately meet your wounded self and welcome the wounds as teachers. It's painful. It's uncomfortable. But it's also really beautiful.

It's honouring and loving yourself and embracing

the parts crying out for attention rather than pushing them away or ignoring them. When we love ourselves, we don't practise self-harm or behaviours that aren't in our best interests.

Imagine for a moment that there's a wounded child knocking on the door of your heart. They're scared, they're hurting, and they're desperately seeking comfort and reassurance.

How would you respond?

Most of us wouldn't hesitate to open that door wide, to wrap our arms around that child, and to offer them all the love and compassion they need. We'd soothe their fears, dry their tears, and remind them that they are safe and loved.

Now, consider this - what if that wounded child is actually a part of yourself?

What if it's the inner child within you, crying out for comfort and understanding?

Would you treat yourself with the same kindness and compassion that you would offer to an external child in need?

It's a powerful question, and one that invites deep self-reflection.

All too often, we're quick to judge ourselves harshly,

to push away our own pain and vulnerability. But what if, instead, we embraced those wounded parts of ourselves with the same tenderness and care that we would offer to others?

By offering ourselves this same level of compassion, we can begin to heal the wounds of the past and nurture a sense of wholeness and self-acceptance. It's not always easy, and it requires practice and patience. But with each act of self-compassion, we take a step closer to embracing our true selves and living from a place of love and authenticity.

When you stop using alcohol or other substances to numb your emotions, it's like removing a mask that you've been wearing for years. Suddenly, you're faced with the raw, unfiltered reality of your emotions, and it can be overwhelming.

At first, it might feel like a floodgate has been opened, and a wave of emotions comes rushing in. You may find yourself grappling with intense feelings of sadness, anger, or anxiety that you've been pushing down for years. It can be disorienting and uncomfortable, but it's also a sign of progress.

These feelings are like signposts along the road

of your recovery, pointing you towards areas of your life that need attention and healing. They may be reminders of past traumas that you've been avoiding or signals that you need to make changes in your current circumstances.

It's important to remember that these feelings, no matter how uncomfortable they may be, are not your enemy. In fact, they're trying to tell you something important. They're urging you to pay attention, to listen to your inner voice, and to take action to address whatever needs to be addressed.

By embracing these feelings as messengers rather than obstacles, you can begin to uncover the underlying issues that have been holding you back and start to move towards true healing and wholeness.

Coming to terms with the reality that alcohol is not your friend can be a profound and liberating moment in your journey towards sobriety. For so long, it may have felt like alcohol was a comforting companion, a way to unwind after a long day or to socialise with friends. But as you've discovered, it's often a false friend, masking deeper issues and ultimately causing more harm than good.

When you reach the point of acceptance, it's like

a veil has been lifted, and you can see things more clearly. You no longer have to expend energy trying to convince yourself that you can moderate your drinking or that alcohol is an essential part of your life. Instead, you can embrace the truth and move forward with clarity and purpose.

Acceptance doesn't mean giving up or resigning yourself to a life without joy or pleasure. On the contrary, it's the first step towards true freedom and happiness. By acknowledging the reality of your relationship with alcohol, you open the door to a world of possibilities. You can explore new interests, cultivate healthier habits, and build deeper connections with yourself and others.

There's a sense of relief that comes with acceptance, a sense of lightness as you release the burden of denial and self-deception. You realise that you no longer have to struggle against your own instincts or justify your choices to yourself or others. You're free to live authentically, guided by your values and aspirations rather than by the demands of addiction.

Avoidance is the opposite of acceptance, and alcohol gets us into the very dangerous pattern of numbing discomfort, making us serial discomfort avoiders. Our need for people and situations to be a certain way for us to be okay can create tension in the mind and body. That alone is enough for some people to want to drink to avoid it.

Fighting against reality can lead to shitty thinking, and shitty thinking can derail you from your path. Worrying and creating stories in your mind won't do you any good.

Tony Robbins says, 'We must stand guard at the door of our mind,' which conjures up visions of a big, burly bouncer standing at the door of a nightclub and booting out the drunken troublemakers.

We need to treat our minds the same way. We are in control of our minds, and we need to remember that we are the ones who let thoughts in and allow them to take up residence there.

Think of your busy mind like an out-of-control Labrador puppy. You can't let him run around everywhere, or there will be utter chaos. Before you know it, your leg will be getting humped, and there will be shit everywhere. The mind is exactly the same. Challenge your thoughts and remember that just because it's a thought doesn't mean it's real.

Alcohol impedes the ability to differentiate between

what's real and what's not. It doesn't allow you to see life as it is, accept it, and take the necessary action. In that sense, alcohol makes us emotional brats because there's less time spent on accepting reality as it is and more time spent in the cycle of party time followed by regrets the following morning.

When we stop fighting life, it becomes an invaluable teacher. It shows us the beauty of going with the flow without constantly fighting against the current. By letting go of the need to control everything, we find a deep sense of peace within ourselves. Embracing life as it comes, without expecting it to fit our desires, brings a newfound freedom and contentment. We discover that true happiness stems from within, regardless of what's happening around us.

So, let's move forward with courage, knowing that each stumble and setback is just another opportunity to learn and grow.

17.
BRINGING IT ALL BACK HOME

Ash : In my first year of quitting alcohol, I was on fire. I wrote a book, recorded an album, and set my career on a whole new path. It was like I had a new superpower. It felt like an unfair advantage.

How had I left it so long?

Why hadn't I done it ten years earlier?

I started to experience a little kick to my cranium, and suddenly, I had access to all my intellectual resources. Gone were the days when I was waking up hungover and making excuses.

When you choose sobriety, you're not just saying no to alcohol. You're saying yes to a life of possibility, purpose, and endless potential. If you make this one decision to quit, you don't have to be tortured with the many micro-decisions.

Saying 'I don't drink' may feel strange in your mouth at first, but once you begin to see and feel the benefits, it tastes SO sweet.

You're freeing up so much space in your life by saying those three little words. For me, that first year felt like a natural high. It's awesome, you become more intelligent, richer, better looking - nowhere near as puffy. I'm not saying there will never be challenges in sobriety, but YOU choose the context and significance of those challenges. If you're going to quit, you might as well make it as enjoyable as possible.

If you feel like alcohol is ruling your life or even just nagging from the corner, then perhaps it's time for change.

Quitting alcohol is a good news story and the best part is that the good news scales.

If you previously drank a bit too much, then quitting will improve your life for sure. However, if you were a complete boozehound fuck up, the news is excellent! Your life is about to get a hell of a lot better!

But first, you have to make the decision to quit. Or else, where is your drinking taking you? Ten years from now, you will arrive...somewhere. Think about that. Things will not be the same as they are now. You will be ten years older for a start, but you will arrive… somewhere.

Where do you want that somewhere to be?

Chances are that 'somewhere' will be at the end of the road that you're currently travelling.

Is that a road you want to continue going down?

In my case, I had gradually been drinking more every successive year. Blacking out. Getting puffy. Experiencing my kids seeing me paralytic (something I thought would never happen). My career was going downhill, and my relationship was suffering. I was heading in a bad direction.

Where would I have arrived?

I hate thinking about it. But it's important to think about it, reflect on where I could have been, and how divergent those two possible paths were.

The last six years have been utterly mind-blowing. I am unapologetic for feeling an even greater sense of optimism for the decades ahead, professionally and personally. I am continually growing. There's no limit to what I can achieve.

This is normal.

This is how it's supposed to be.

It's just that I was wasting half my life by being

wasted.

Imagine getting twenty hours a week bonus life back just by quitting! It's literally bonus life! Like a genie granting you an extra twenty quality years. Think about what you could do with all that extra time.

You could spend it soaking up every precious moment with your kids, watching them grow and thrive right before your eyes. Or maybe you'll finally dive headfirst into that hobby or passion project you've been putting off for far too long.

Learning something new becomes a breeze when you've got those extra hours at your disposal. It's like the universe is nudging you towards growth and discovery, whispering in your ear that the world is full of endless possibilities.

But perhaps the most liberating part of reclaiming those twenty bonus hours a week is the chance to live life on your own terms.

No longer shackled by the constraints of alcohol, you're free to embrace your true, authentic self and carve out a path that's uniquely yours. So go ahead, seize the day, and be the authentic individual you were meant to be without being homogenised by a beverage.

★ ★ ★

Danni: I used to think alcohol was how I had fun - now, there's no longer a price to pay for my 'fun.' I can't believe I am saying this, but now, for fun, I jump in freezing cold ice baths, do yoga and meditation, wake up at five in the morning to watch the sunrise, and work on myself... all of that to me is fun with a capital F. Because now I see the things that make me truly happy and fulfilled as fun. Waking up hungover and hating myself is NOT fun.

Alcohol has no power over me anymore, which is an incredible feeling. It's an empowering choice to step away from its influence.

Doing the deeper work on myself and understanding my emotional triggers, patterns, and behaviours was not always easy, and I didn't expect it to be. As I always say, nothing great has ever come out of a comfort zone.

Working on your relationship with yourself is a lifelong work in progress. All or nothing is a way many of us over-drinkers are. This quality can be good, especially if we send that energy towards constructive endeavours rather than destructive behaviours. That's what keeps me from listening to the voice in my head telling me I can 'have just one' drink.

After all this work I've done on myself, it's not worth

risking it. I could end up right back where I started, and nothing is worth that.

I couldn't stand to live that life now. I feel sad for that version of myself when I look back, and it breaks my heart to see how much I was avoiding and hurting myself in the process. The old me was so full of self-loathing, but I truly love who I am now.

I didn't know then, but my binge drinking was powered by a desire to fit in, to be accepted and loved. That desire was born from old childhood wounds, a bottomless longing in me that I have realised only I can fill. No external substance or person can ever do that.

I don't blame anyone in my childhood for that, but I can see how that old wound inside me created so much destructive behaviour. Now, through doing the work on myself, I am aware of when that wound shows up. I can ask myself what part of me needs to be soothed rather than drowning it out.

If you're sober, you have to learn to sit with your discomforts, to feel your way through them. We all have our own scars, our own battle wounds from navigating this crazy thing called life. It doesn't matter who you are or even how happy your childhood was - nobody comes through life unscathed. We all carry around these little nuggets of pain, these core beliefs about ourselves that we've been lugging around since who knows when.

But here's where it gets interesting - giving up alcohol is like peeling back the layers of an onion and finally seeing yourself for who you really are. It's like shining a spotlight on those dark corners of your mind and realising that, hey, maybe there's some work to be done here.

It's hard work and can be extremely uncomfortable at times. But here's the thing - when you sit with that discomfort and feel your way through it, that's where the magic happens. That's where the real growth occurs.

So, embrace the discomfort, lean into the pain, and watch as you emerge on the other side, stronger, wiser, and more resilient than ever before.

Isn't it wild to think that by simply letting go of alcohol, you're opening the floodgates to a world of healing, growth, and happiness? It's like stumbling upon a hidden treasure trove right in your own backyard.

The impact of your decision to quit reaches far beyond just you. Sure, you're the one taking the plunge, but your choices extend to everyone around you - your kids, your friends, your family, and even your future descendants.

By choosing sobriety, you're not just changing your own life - you're rewriting the script for generations to come. You're setting an example, showing your loved ones what it means to live authentically, to prioritise your health and well-being, and to chase after your dreams with unwavering determination.

The choices you make become the life you create, and they will have a ripple effect, so make your choices good ones.

Ten years from now, you will arrive... somewhere.

Where do you want that somewhere to be?

ACKNOWLEDGEMENTS

We'd like to acknowledge Danni's BFF, Lisa Candy, who was the one who said, 'I'm going to take a year off' and started this whole thing. Also Scott Owen and Claire Rantall who joined our little 'Club Sober' WhatsApp group. We didn't know it then but some pretty amazing things were set in motion the moment we set that group up, I don't know if we could've done it without you.

Danni: Thanks to Ash for being right there in the trenches with me, for going along with some of my 'woo woo' ideas, your wisdom and your courage to keep on evolving is inspiring, how lucky I am to be married to my best friend. To all my friends and family who accepted me without the booze, I know it was a big shift. To people like Lissie Turner, Ben Schiller, and the other ex-trashbags who were a beacon of light and inspiration. To Lyndal Hunt, who I have known for most of my life and who is my absolute hero in sobriety.

To Katelyn Rew, thank you for your insights and editing prowess. To Luke Sniewski, Mark Purser, Nick

Hanlon, Nathan Carr and Donna Gee. To every guest on my podcast who helped to make the show such a huge success, you inspire me with your stories, bravery and wisdom. To the listeners of the podcast whose messages motivate me to keep going. To the HIQA community and Grads group, I bloody love you guys. You are all my heroes, and working with you is an honour.

★ ★ ★

Ash: Thanks to my best friend and wife, Danni, for sharing every moment on this journey, including introducing me to the (then) unthinkable idea that you were quitting alcohol. I was following you into battle, but I needed it more than you did. I shudder to think where I would be, where we would be, and where my career would be if you hadn't come home and told me you were quitting for a year.

★ ★ ★

Our sobriety has been the gift that has kept on giving. I've loved sharing the spiritual journey you've been on since that first year, and you never stopped. You've been compounding that growth every year over the last six years, and it's been an amazing thing to sit back and watch you use that wisdom to help thousands of people! And your 'woo woo' stuff set me on a path to manifest my dreams, so I'm a convert.

Speaking of 'woo woo,' thanks to Steph Gilmore for the interview that confirmed for me that it's possible to manifest your dreams on purpose. There is nothing like hearing it from an eight-time surfing world champ. Thanks to all the amazing people I interviewed in Surf by Day, Jam by Night. It feels like fate that the writing of this book happened in my first year of sobriety. It wasn't lost on me that a freak of nature like Kelly Slater was never a party animal. In fact, when he first came on the scene, it was kinda controversial that he was sober. Sounds funny now, but it was an act of rebellion to 'not' be a trashbag when he hit the professional circuit.

As I continued writing the book, interviewing Jack Johnson, Pete Murrey, and Dave Rastavitch, I realised they're not trashbags. They have that side in check. It was an influential time, and it helped bolster my resolution to stay on this path, so thank you.

BOOKS BY THIS AUTHOR

Surf by Day, Jam by Night is seasoned bluesman and surfer Ash Grunwald's deep dive into the extraordinary.

Ash takes to the road, interviewing fifteen of the world's top surfer-musicians. From Kelly Slater to Stephanie Gilmore, Jack Johnson to Dave Rastovich, Pete Murray to G. Love, and many more, these are people doing life their own way, like Ash.

Soulful and candid, these conversations offer insights into the lives and minds of some masters of both surfing and music. Spanning stories of heavy wipe-outs and heaving crowds, riffs on style, the flow state, career longevity and jamming vs shredding, this book is an often light-hearted, wide-ranging meditation on what it really takes to live your dreams.

If you've ever found yourself in any kind of rut and wondered if there's something more out there, here's a call to wake up, take your life into your hands and dare to follow your passions.

ABOUT THE AUTHOR

Danni Carr is the host of the hugely popular *'How I Quit Alcohol'* Podcast, a sobriety coach and mentor. In 2020, she completed Compassionate Inquiry Studies for Professionals with Dr Gabor Maté and became a qualified breathwork and meditation teacher in 2023. Danni has worked with hundreds of people to help them understand their triggers, behaviours, and coping mechanisms. She facilitates this help via one-on-one coaching, the HIQA transformation challenge, and national and international retreats.

ABOUT THE AUTHOR

Musician, songwriter, guitarist, author, and podcaster Ash Grunwald has enjoyed a prolific career spanning twenty years, with twelve studio albums, six Australian Top 50 albums, multiple ARIA nominations, and two APRA Awards. Known for collaborations with top Australian artists like Josh Teskey and Kasey Chambers, his album *'Push The Blues Away'* hit #8 on the ARIA charts. He has supported legends like James Brown and The Black Keys, played sold-out festivals worldwide, and performed at Bluesfest ten times. In 2019, he published *'Surf by Day, Jam by Night,'* featuring interviews with Kelly Slater and Jack Johnson, and launched the podcast 'Soulful Conversations,' hosting guests like John Butler and Missy Higgins.

www.ingramcontent.com/pod-product-compliance
Lightning Source LLC
Chambersburg PA
CBHW030428010526
44109CB00053B/1066